British
Horse
Society

THE BHS COMPLETE TRAINING MANUAL FOR

STAGE 2

Islay Auty FBHS

Updated and revised by
Margaret Linington-Payne MA (Ed) BHSI

KENILWORTH PRESS

Copyright © 2013 The British Horse Society

First published in the UK in 2004 under the title *The BHS Training Manual for Stage 2*
Updated and expanded as *The BHS Complete Training Manual for Stage 2* published in 2009
by Kenilworth Press, an imprint of Quiller Publishing Ltd
This second edition published 2013

British Library Cataloguing-in-Publication Data
  A catalogue record for this book
  is available from the British Library

ISBN 978 1 905693 61 0

Line drawings by Dianne Breeze
Book and cover design by Sharyn Troughton
Printed in Malta by Gutenberg Press Ltd

Kenilworth Press

An imprint of Quiller Publishing
Wykey House, Wykey, Shrewsbury, SY4 1JA
Tel: 01939 261616 Fax: 01939 261606
E-mail: info@quillerbooks.com
Website: www.kenilworthpress.co.uk

THE BHS COMPLETE TRAINING MANUAL FOR

STAGE 2

NOTES FOR STUDENTS

This training manual provides a comprehensive guide to the techniques, knowledge and understanding required to prepare for the BHS Stage 2 examination.

Contents

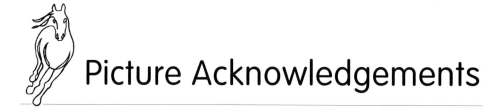

Picture Acknowledgements

All line drawings are by Dianne Breeze, with the exception of those on pages 65, 136–7, which are by Carole Vincer.

Picture sources

The author and publishers wish to acknowledge the following books as sources for some of the illustrations:

- *The BHS Complete Manual of Equitation*, Consultant Editor Patrick Print OBE FBHS, published by Kenilworth Press

- *The BHS Complete Manual of Stable Management Second Edition*, Revised and updated by Josephine Batty-Smith BHSI, published by Kenilworth Press

- *The BHS Veterinary Manual*, by P. Stewart Hastie MRCVS, published by Kenilworth Press

- *Learn to Ride with The British Horse Society*, by Islay Auty FBHS, published by Kenilworth Press

- *Lungeing and Long-Reining*, by Jennie Loriston-Clarke FBHS, published by Kenilworth Press

- *Threshold Picture Guide No. 8, Field Management*, by Mary Gordon Watson, published by Kenilworth Press

- *Threshold Picture Guide No. 43, Functional Anatomy*, by Dr Chris Colles BVetMed, PhD, MRCVS, published by Kenilworth Press

How to Use This Book

The aim of this book is to provide students working towards Stage 2 with detailed guidance to help prepare thoroughly for the examination. The information is laid out as follows:

Each topic has a section on **'What the assessor is looking for'**, which gives a fuller picture of the level of information required or what you might be asked to do.

The sections entitled **'How to become competent'** give you the knowledge and practical skills required to be successful.

Throughout, the book is aiming to clearly outline the requirements of the syllabus, and give you a sound basis of the knowledge required.

The sections on gaining competence should be sufficiently flexible for you to be able to adapt the requirements to your own situation with horses. Whatever that situation may be, you must demonstrate a certain speed and efficiency which would be appropriate to your competence for working in the industry and maintaining credibility at Stage 2 level.

A Stage 2 worker should be capable of looking after stabled horses and those at grass, with competence and efficiency within a relevant timescale appropriate to the experience at this level. As a Stage 2 worker you should be capable of independent, self-motivated work on a day-to-day basis, but there should always be a more senior member of staff to whom you can turn for advice if necessary, or in the event of an emergency.

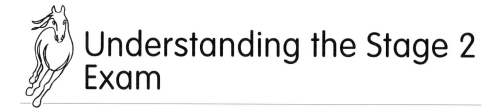

Understanding the Stage 2 Exam

After Stage 1

You will have achieved BHS Stage 1 through one of two routes: either you worked steadily through levels 1–6 of the Society's Progressive Riding Tests (PRTs) in your regular lessons at a BHS-Approved Riding Establishment; or you chose to sit the BHS Stage 1 examination and were successful in passing the Horse Knowledge and Care section and the Riding section, which combine to give you the BHS Stage 1 qualification. Whichever of these pathways you chose, you are now in a position to consider aiming for BHS Stage 2.

When working toward an examination, whatever the standard or subject, it is essential to consolidate the knowledge required at that level. This gives you confidence and assurance in your skills, which in turn promotes motivation to seek further ability and competence at a higher level.

Think in terms of developing experience and ability alongside further training, gradually moving yourself toward the expertise required at the next level of examination. You should then be capable of taking and passing the Stage 2 exam.

Requirements of Stage 2

The candidate must hold either BHS Stage 1 or the Progressive Riding Tests 1–6 inclusive as a prerequisite for applying to take Stage 2. If you hold NVQ Level 2 Horse Care (riding/schooling horses under supervision) (Unit 2/3) you are entitled to have direct entry to Stage 2 or Stage 3.

The candidate must understand the general management and requirements of horses for their health and well-being. Working under regular but not constant supervision, the candidate should be able to carry out the care of stabled and grass-kept horses during all seasons of the year. He/she must have an understanding of how the horse adjusts his balance to carry a rider. The candidate must be capable of riding an experienced horse or pony in the countryside and on the public highway as well as in a manège, or indoor school.

- It is possible to study for and achieve Stage 2 if you are a committed amateur rider who spends a lot of time around horses as well as riding several times a week.

- It is also possible to work for Stage 2 if you own your own horse and have some guidance in your riding (perhaps regular lessons or training at Riding Club clinics with an instructor who is BHS qualified, and who understands the requirements of the BHS Stage exams).

- It is probably easiest to work for Stage 2 if you are in a regular training situation (either at college or a commercial establishment where students are trained for BHS exams).

- Whatever your chosen pathway towards Stage 2, remember that it is a standard that begins to expect a confirmed practical ability in certain tasks of horsemastership and riding, and these can only be achieved by **practice**.

Riding and Road Safety Test

The Riding and Road Safety Certificate is a prerequisite for the riding section of the Stage 2 exam.

The aim of the Riding and Road Safety Test is, in conjunction with the Highway Code, to promote responsible, considerate and courteous riding on the public highway by all riders.

In these days of ever-increasing traffic volumes on the public highway, it is essential that every rider takes responsibility for his or her own safety on the road and maintains courtesy towards and understanding of other road users. The Society's well-respected Riding and Road Safety Test has been taken by thousands of riders and is a tangible way of addressing every rider's safety on the public highways.

If you are on a training course as a full-time student, it is almost certain that those in charge of your training will 'build in' the road safety training and test in the preparation for your Stage 2.

If you are working for your Stage 2 independently then there are various ways you can find out about the availability of and training for Riding and Road Safety Tests in your area. You can contact:

- The Examinations Office at The British Horse Society (see page 205 for address) for details of local contacts.

- Your Regional or County Road Safety Officer, who will tell you of courses and tests in your area.

The BHS publishes a very comprehensive 'Riding and Road Safety Manual'. Called *Riding and Roadcraft*, this book is essential reading for anyone training for the test. The manual should be read in conjunction with a current copy of *The Highway Code*, which has a section specifically dedicated to horses on the road. While it is not compulsory, it is strongly recommended that riders receive a minimum of eight hours tuition from a BHS-Approved Safety Trainer before they undertake the test.

The Test

This is divided into two units:

- The theory test. A multiple-choice question paper.

- The simulated road test. A controlled, simulated test. If the candidate is successful here, this is followed by the test on the public highway. This is an individual test on the road.

On achievement of the Riding and Road Safety Test, your certificate **MUST** be sent into the Exams Office with your Stage 2 application. If the exam date has been applied for before you take the test, then you **MUST** take the certificate to the Stage 2 exam: the chief assessor will need to see it before allowing you to take the riding section of Stage 2.

If you have made every effort to take your test before your Stage 2 then dispensation may be given for you to take your Stage 2 prior to taking the test, as long as a test date is booked. This dispensation is not automatic and must be applied for.

Practical application

Reference has already been made to the practical ability that you must achieve for Stage 2 level. As you read this book and each section is explained, it is essential that you are very familiar with each unit. Below are listed ways in which your practical skills may be developed if you are not in a regular 'working with horses' environment.

- Spend **at least** one **full** day a week working in a yard where horses are kept both stabled and at grass.

- Make sure that your work is observed and supervised by someone who can advise you on safe and good practice.

- If you care for your own horse (e.g. DIY livery), try to follow a system of good practice and if possible ask someone to observe some of the tasks you do (e.g. tacking up or grooming) on a regular basis and accept their constructive criticism.

- Spend one day a week in a 'day-release' training situation, where you can undergo training and carry out supervised yard-work practice.

When carrying out any task, being able 'to do it' does not necessarily demonstrate professional competence in an exam situation. It is essential that the way you 'do it' underlines your awareness of good and safe practice, and is a skill that you could transfer to someone else with less competence. By copying you they would develop good practice themselves and not be put at risk by following your example and method.

Your practical application (of tasks) must be:

- Safe.

- In the interests of the horse's welfare.

- Completed efficiently and in a reasonable timescale.

- An acceptable method for someone else to copy or learn from.

There is no substitute for practice. Knowledge of the subject must be thorough and sufficient for the level required, but practical competence is vital.

STAGE 2

EQL Level 2 Diploma in BHS Horse Knowledge and Care

IMPORTANT: Candidates are advised to check that they are working from the latest examination syllabus, as examination content and procedure are liable to alteration. Contact the BHS Examinations Office for up-to-date information regarding the syllabus.

# Syllabus

Candidates must be physically fit in order to carry out yard and fieldwork efficiently, without undue stress and strain. They will be expected to demonstrate competent use of time.

UNIT 1a
Groom and Plait Horses and Fit Equipment
10 credits/75 guided learning hours

Unit purpose and aims
Learners will be able to safely and competently handle a horse in order to undertake well defined tasks to the standard required by industry at this level. They will know and be able to select and use relevant equipment to strap a horse (including banging); plait a mane and tail and fit appropriate equipment for travelling. Learners must show an efficient use of time for this level as required by industry. They will display a level of competence and autonomy for entry into employment, and/or skills progression.

Learner Outcomes		Assessment Criteria	
The learner will:		The learner can:	
1.	Be able to work safely and efficiently	1.1	Use handling and working procedures, maintaining health, safety and welfare of self, others and horses at all times
		1.2	Maintain a clean working environment for self, others, horses and equipment
		1.3	Use time efficiently accordingly to industry practice
2.	Know procedures for working safely on a yard	2.1	Describe the actions to be taken in the event of an accident on the yard
		2.2	Describe ways of working safely on the yard
3.	Be able to strap a horse	3.1	Select and use equipment for grooming fit horses
		3.2	Use equipment to assist the development of muscle tone
4.	Know the process of grooming a rugged up horse	4.1	Outline how to groom a stabled horse prior to /after exercise
5.	Be able to plait the mane and tail with elastic bands/thread	5.1	Prepare the mane and tail for plaiting
		5.2	Put plaits in to a mane using bands/thread
		5.3	Plait a tail using bands/thread
6.	Be able to prepare a horse for travelling	6.1	Select and fit equipment suitable for travelling a horse relevant for the distance travelled and weather conditions
		6.2	Fit a travel bandage and travel boot
7.	Know procedures for fitting and storing clothing and equipment	7.1	Describe why it is important to fit clothing and travelling equipment
		7.2	Describe methods for washing clothing and equipment
		7.3	Describe how to store clothing and equipment when not in use
		7.4	Describe methods for maintaining clothing and equipment in good condition

Candidates will be expected to give practical demonstrations as well as be involved in discussion of selected tasks and topics.

If you have recently read the BHS Training Manual for Stage 1, or you have taken the Stage 1 exam within the last twelve months, you will already be familiar with the format of the syllabus (which changed in 2011). For those of you who have not seen the syllabus in this format before, a little explanation will reassure you that the standard and requirements of Stage 2 are unchanged.

UNIT 1b
Fit, remove and maintain tack for exercise
3 credits/23 guided learning hours

Unit purpose and aims
The aim and purpose of this unit provides the learner with the knowledge and skills to tack up and un-tack horses for exercise. The learner will need to be fully aware of the importance of health and safety in connection with this work and will need to be able to recognise hazards and assess risks.

Learner Outcomes	Assessment Criteria	
The learner will:	The learner can:	
1. Be able to fit and remove tack for exercise	1.1	Prepare and control the horse in preparation for tacking up
	1.2	Fit suitable tack for exercise including: i) bridles ii) martingales iii) saddles iv) nosebands and bits v) breastplate
	1.3	Fit suitable boots for exercise
	1.4	Remove equipment after exercise and store tack safely and correctly
2. Be able to work safely	2.1	Work in a way which maintains health and safety and security of horse, self and others during work which is consistent with relevant legislation, codes of practice and any additional requirements
3. Be able to select, use and maintain tack	3.1	Select and check tack for safety and suitability for the specified work
	3.2	Clean, maintain and store tack in a safe and effective working condition
4. Know how to fit tack and remove for exercise	4.1	State the reasons for checking tack for comfort and safety
	4.2	Identify a range of tack in common use and how to fit
	4.3	Describe the problems which may occur when tacking up or untacking
	4.4	Describe how to recognise ill-fitting tack and the appropriate action to take
	4.5	Describe the procedure for untacking a horse safely and securely and the purpose of checking condition of horse after untacking
	4.6	Describe the reasons for checking, cleaning, maintaining and storing tack and the actions to take if tack is found to be unsafe
5. Know relevant health and safety legislation	5.1	Outline the current health and safety legislation, codes of practice and any additional requirements

The BHS Complete Training Manual for Stage 2

The syllabus is clearly divided into units. You may take the whole exam on the same day or choose to take one or more units at a time.

UNIT 2a
The Principles of Horse Health and Anatomy
8 credits/60 guided learning hours

Unit purpose and aims
Learners will know the structure of the skeleton. Using a live horse they will be able to identify its skeletal structure including parts of the foot. They will know the position of the main internal organs and the structure of the digestive system. They will also know about horse health and condition and understand the importance of keeping records and regular worming. They will know how to treat minor wounds and care for sick horses. Learners will exhibit a level of knowledge and understanding required by industry for entry into employment, and or knowledge progression.

Learner Outcomes		Assessment Criteria	
The learner will:		The learner can:	
1.	Know the horse's skeleton	1.1	Identify the horse's bones
2.	Know the structure, function and potential problems of the horse's foot	2.1	Describe the external parts of the horse's foot
		2.2	Explain the functions and importance of the parts of the foot
		2.3	Describe the problems associated with long feet
3.	Know the position of the horse's main internal organs	3.1	Indicate the position of internal organs on a horse
4.	Know the basic structure of the horse's digestive system	4.1	Describe the horses digestive system
		4.2	Describe the function of the horse's digestive system
		4.3	Describe why 'bulk' is important to the system
5.	Know how to recognise a horse's health, welfare and condition	5.1	Give the horse's normal Temperature, Pulse and Respiration rate
		5.2	Describe how the horse's stance and bodily functions indicate its state of health and well-being
		5.3	Describe signs of poor health in a horse
		5.4	Describe signs of unsoundness in a horse
		5.5	Describe signs of a horse having problems with its teeth
6.	Know how to recognise and treat minor wounds	6.1	Differentiate between types of minor wounds
		6.2	Describe how to treat minor wounds
		6.3	Give instances of when a vet may need to be called
7.	Know how to care for sick horses	7.1	Describe the principles of sick nursing
8.	Know the importance of keeping horse records	8.1	Describe the reasons for keeping health records
9.	Know the importance of worming	9.1	Describe the indications of worm infestation in the horse
		9.2	Describe how a worming programme is devised

Make sure that you are confident and competent in all areas of the requirements. There should be nothing within the syllabus that you have never heard of!

UNIT 2b
The Principles of Shoeing, Clipping and Trimming Horses
4 credits/30 guided learning hours

Unit purpose and aims
Learners will know and understand the procedures for clipping, trimming and shoeing horses. Learners will know the importance of efficient use of time and exhibit a level of understanding required by industry for entry into employment, and or knowledge progression.

Learner Outcomes		Assessment Criteria	
The learner will:		The learner can:	
1.	Know the reasons for clipping and relevant welfare issues	1.1	Describe why and when horses may be clipped
		1.2	Describe welfare implications of clipping
		1.3	Differentiate between types of clip
2.	Know how to assemble and maintain clippers	2.1	Describe how to assemble clippers
		2.2	Describe checks required before clipping
		2.3	Describe the maintenance of clippers during and after clipping
		2.4	Outline the potential dangers of clipping and how to minimise them
3.	Know why and how to pull manes and tails	3.1	Describe how, why and when to trim and pull a mane
		3.2	Describe how, why and when to pull a tail
		3.3	Outline when you would not pull a mane or tail
4.	Know why and how to trim horses	4.1	Describe how, why and when to trim a tail
		4.2	Describe how, why and when to trim other parts of the horse's body
		4.3	Outline when you would not trim a horse
		4.4	Outline different ways of trimming
5.	Know the procedure for shoeing, including the use of the farriers tools	5.1	Describe reasons for shoeing horses
		5.2	Describe the procedure for shoeing a horse
		5.3	Describe the well shod foot
		5.4	List the farriers tools and their use
6.	Know the procedure for removing a twisted shoe in an emergency	6.1	Explain how to remove a twisted shoe in an emergency

Each unit is allocated a level of credit. One unit of credit is worth ten hours of study. So if a unit is worth three credits you should expect to study for about thirty hours to become proficient.

UNIT 3a
The Principles of Watering, Feeding and Fittening Horses
6 credits/45 guided learning hours

Unit purpose and aims
Learners will know and understand the principles of providing water and feed to different types of horse. They will also know how to get an unfit horse fit for regular work and 'rough off', relating these to feeding and health care. Learners will exhibit a level of knowledge and understanding required by industry for entry into employment, and or knowledge progression.

Learner Outcomes	Assessment Criteria	
The learner will:	The learner can:	
1. Know the rules of watering and understand their reasons	1.1	State the rules of watering
	1.2	Explain the reasons behind the rules of watering
	1.3	Describe different ways of providing water for horses
2. Know the rules of feeding and understand their reasons	2.1	State the rules of feeding
	2.2	Explain the reasons behind the rules of feeding
3. Know a variety of feedstuffs, their preparation and suitability for horses	3.1	Recognise and assess feed samples, their quality and describe their preparation
	3.2	Identify feedstuffs that have a 'heating' or fattening effect on horses
	3.3	Identify feedstuffs suitable for a variety of horses
4. Know about feeding bulk food	4.1	Describe reasons for soaking hay
	4.2	Describe alternatives to hay and their nutritional differences
5. Know how to produce a feed chart	5.1	Identify the reasons for producing a feed chart
	5.2	Identify ways of producing a feed chart
6. Know how to get a turned away horse fit for non stressful exercise up to one and a half hours a day	6.1	Describe a fittening programme for bringing up a horse from grass into regular work
	6.2	Describe possible health and welfare implications when bringing up a horse from grass
	6.3	Describe feeding in relation to the fittening programme
	6.4	Identify possible causes of concussion and strain in the horse when riding out
	6.5	Describe possible behavioural changes in the horse when riding out alone or in company
7. Know how to care for a horse after work	7.1	Describe a procedure for cooling a horse off after work
	7.2	Outline and explain the importance of the care of the horse after work
8. Know how to 'rough off' a horse	8.1	Describe a suitable programme for roughing off a horse

All work that was required at Stage 1 should now be seen to be carried out to a higher standard of efficiency. Candidates should show an increasing awareness of the needs of the horse(s) in their care and the importance of co-operating and communicating with fellow workers. In addition candidates will be expected to show knowledge and practical ability in all the subjects.

UNIT 3b
The Principles of Stabling and Grassland Care for Horses
5 credits/38 guided learning hours

Unit purpose and aims
Learners will know and understand the principles of horse behaviour and caring for horses when stabled and at grass. They will also be able to discuss stable design and construction and pasture management. Learners will exhibit a level of knowledge and understanding required by industry for entry into employment, and or knowledge progression.

Learner Outcomes		Assessment Criteria	
The learner will:		The learner can:	
1.	Know the requirements for stable design and construction	1.1	Describe stable design and dimensions for horses and ponies
		1.2	Describe materials for stable construction
		1.3	Explain the importance of good ventilation and ways this may be provided
		1.4	Explain the importance of good drainage and how this may be provided
		1.5	Describe various stable fixtures and fittings
2.	Know about horse behaviour and welfare when stabled	2.1	Describe how stabling would affect a horse's natural lifestyle and how this can be minimised
		2.2	Describe how to accommodate a new horse
		2.3	Identify signs of nervous or undesirable behaviour in a stabled horse
		2.4	Describe how to handle nervous or undesirable behaviour in a stabled horse
3.	Know the requirements for grassland care and pasture maintenance	3.1	Describe the ideal requirements and features for horse pasture
		3.2	Describe how to maintain good quality grazing
		3.3	List and describe plants that are poisonous to horses
4.	Know about horse behaviour and welfare when at grass	4.1	Describe causes of unsettled behaviour in horses at grass and list some causes for this
		4.2	Explain why horses may be difficult to catch

UNIT 4
Lunge a horse under supervision
4 credits/30 guided learning hours

Unit purpose and aims
The aim if this unit is to provide the learner with the skills and knowledge for lungeing a horse under supervision. It includes checking and fitting suitable tack and the conditions which may affect the process. The learner will need to be fully aware of the importance of health and safety in connection with this work and will need to be able to recognise hazards and assess risks.

Learner Outcomes	Assessment Criteria	
The learner will:	The learner can:	
1. Be able to lunge a horse	1.1	Check that the lunge area is suitable for the exercise
	1.2	Wear the appropriate protective clothing
	1.3	Select, check and fit suitable lunge tack and equipment according to instructions
	1.4	Maintain control of the horse at all times appropriate to the conditions
	1.5	Lunge the horse according to instructions
	1.6	Remove tack and maintain security and safety of horse throughout
2. Be able to work safely	2.1	Work in a way which maintains health and safety and is consistent with current codes of practice and any additional requirements
3. Know how to lunge horses	3.1	State the reasons why lungeing can be substituted for ridden exercise
	3.2	Describe procedures associated with lungeing horses
	3.3	List types and use of equipment and protective clothing
	3.4	Describe the ways in which conditions, such as; weather, surface and other horses affect the process
	3.5	Explain the lungeing process and how to recognise and deal with problems
4. Know the current health and safety legislation	4.1	Outline the current health and safety legislation, codes of practice and any additional requirements, which apply to this area of work

UNIT 1a

Groom and Plait Horses and Fit Equipment

10 Credits

# Grooming

Strap a horse; plait the mane and tail

Know:

The process of grooming a rugged-up horse

There are three main types of grooming:

Brushing off

There are two meanings to this term:

(1) A final groom at the end of the day.

(2) The quick tidy-up of a grass-kept horse/pony to make him presentable for exercise.

Quartering

This is the initial groom of the day for a stable-kept horse. The name 'quartering' comes from the way in which the rug is moved on the horse. After the horse is tied up and the feet picked out, the rug is undone and then the front half is folded back to expose the near and offside front 'quarters' of the horse to be brushed off. The rug is then brought forward and the back half is folded forward to expose the hindquarters of the horse, ready to be quickly brushed off. The body brush and curry comb should be used for this. The mane and tail are also brushed out and the eyes, nostrils and dock should be sponged off. If there are any stable stains these should be washed off with a water brush or damp sponge. This procedure is to tidy up the horse ready for exercise and should only take ten to fifteen minutes.

Strapping

This is the full grooming of a stable-kept horse and is usually undertaken after exercise, when the pores of the horse's skin are open and more dirt and grease can be removed. Strapping can take between forty minutes and an hour and includes banging or wisping.

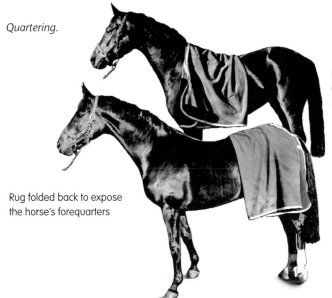

Quartering.

Rug folded forward to expose the horse's hindquarters

Rug folded back to expose the horse's forequarters

Procedure for strapping

- Collect all the equipment you need and prepare the area you will be working in. (It may be useful to remove any water buckets.)

- Put on the horse's headcollar and tie him up safely with a quick-release knot that is neither too tight nor too loose.

- Pick out the horse's feet into a skip. If the feet are muddy after work then wash them. If this is done in the stable, hold the foot over a bucket of water and scrub it clean, using a stiff brush that you dip frequently into the water. Do not wet the foot above the bulbs of the heel as you could cause cracking of the skin in this area.

- If the weather is warm, remove the horse's rugs. If it is cold, it is better to fold back the rugs to help to keep him warm.

- Remove dry mud and sweat with a rubber curry comb or cactus cloth. Use them in a circular motion following the lie of the coat.

- To clean the coat use a body brush in conjunction with a metal curry comb. It is usual always to brush with the hand closer to the horse so you are in a good position to watch his hindquarters. Use long, vigorous strokes, brushing in the direction of the hair. Push the mane over to the non-usual side to ensure you can clean the crest thoroughly. Clean the body brush with the curry comb every two or three strokes. The curry comb should be cleaned out by knocking it on the floor to remove the dust and dead skin.

- To brush the legs, put the curry comb down somewhere safe. Crouch down and brush the outside of the leg you are closest to and the inside of the opposite leg. You can then see what you are doing and how efficient your work is. With the hind legs it may be useful to put the hand you are not brushing with on the horse's quarters to steady him or, if he is quite restless, then hold the tail.

- Use the body brush to brush the mane. Brush a few hairs at a time making sure you are working your way to the bottom of the mane. If the mane is thick then start by pushing it all to the non-usual side again as you did to brush the crest (as per Stage 1).

- Brush the tail out in the same safe way as you learned for Stage 1. If the tail is thin then just use your fingers and not the body brush.

- Brush the head, making sure you undo the headcollar rope and leave it through the string. Slip the headcollar round the horse's neck and gently brush the head with the body brush. Use your spare hand to steady his head. Replace the headcollar and re-tie the quick-release knot.

- Banging or wisping is most commonly done to competition horses in hard work and show animals. It helps to build up muscle tone. Not everybody nowadays bangs their horses. It is undertaken on the muscled parts of the horse – the neck, shoulder and quarters. It should never be done on the bony parts of the body. A horse must get used to being banged, so when trying it on a new (strange) horse start gently and build up the force as he becomes used to it. Take the wisp or massage pad in the hand nearer the horse and a stable rubber in the other. It is necessary to build up a rhythm of banging the muscle and wiping with the stable rubber. If you get into a rhythm the muscle will start to contract as you bang and this will encourage blood supply to the area and build up muscle.

- The horse's eyes, nose and dock need to be sponged. When you have brushed the head you can take one of the sponges and carefully sponge his eyes and nose. After this you can replace the headcollar correctly. You need now to sponge his dock. Take the other sponge and stand in the same position as you would for brushing the tail, lift the tail and wipe the area positively.

- You may well wish to lay the mane with a water brush and put on a tail bandage to lay the tail.

- A final polish can be achieved by wiping the horse over with a stable rubber that is very lightly dampened, if required.

Safety when grooming

Whenever you are grooming a horse, you must be aware of your own safety and that of the horse. Make sure that you stand in a safe position and be aware of the horse's reactions at all times. Prepare the grooming area beforehand (as discussed in Stage 1) and keep the grooming kit out of harm's way while you work.

After-work care

After work it is important that a horse cools down gradually to his normal body temperature so that his metabolism has the chance to recover without further stress.

If the horse is at a competition, loosen the girth and the noseband and walk him until his breathing returns to normal. Walking will help him to regain his breath quicker and will also help him not to stiffen up. The saddle should be left on for the first few minutes so there is time for the blood vessels to refill before the back is exposed to the air when the saddle is removed. A cooler rug can be put over the saddle if the weather is cold. If it is not cold, a rug may not be necessary. Test the horse's temperature by feeling the base of his ears, which should not feel over-hot. If you have been out hacking or hunting, walking the horse home or to the lorry may be enough to complete this part of the cooling-down process.

A small amount of water (about ½ gallon/2.25l) with the chill taken off can be offered to the horse once he is cool. Also after he has cooled down the tack can be removed and he can be washed down. Warm water and a sponge should be used and a sweat-scraper used to remove any excess water. A cooler rug should then be applied

25

and the horse walked round again until dry. He can again be offered a small amount of water with the chill taken off.

The horse must be inspected for injury. Feel his legs for any new lumps and bumps and trot him up to test for lameness. He can then be rugged up and left with a drink and a haynet. He could be given a hard feed after about a further hour. Nowadays most people give the normal feed, although the amount may be a little smaller if the horse is having a day off the next day. Keep an eye on the horse to ensure he does not start sweating again (known as breaking out).

The next day it is important to check the horse over for injury again. There could be a delay in a lump coming up or a lameness showing. He needs to be trotted up to check for soundness, and it is always a good idea to keep a careful watch on his behaviour. If he appears out of character there could be something wrong with him. If all appears fine he will probably enjoy some time relaxing in a field before he starts his work regime again.

Plaiting the mane

- Make sure you have all the equipment you need in your pocket – mane comb, scissors, thread, and rubber bands if using them. Thread the needle before starting to plait and push it through your jumper/waistcoat/jacket, ready to use. If you are going to use a needle rather than bands then it might be an idea to suggest you move the horse outside so that if you drop the needle you will not lose it in the horse's bed. Try very hard not to lose the needle if you are using one. It will appear quite inefficient and is a potential danger to the horse. If you need to stand on something to reach the mane then make sure you choose a safe box, and that you take it into the stable very carefully, watching the horse's reaction. Take a bucket partially filled with water and a water brush into the stable with you. It is easier to plait a damp mane.

- The number of plaits you put in the mane depends on the horse you are plaiting and the job for which he is being plaited. The general rule is that there should be an odd number of plaits down the neck (which stops the neck looking as if it is split into two halves), making an even number in total with the forelock plait. The plaits must, however, all be the same size and, if plaiting the whole mane, use the mane comb to section it out, possibly using the mane comb as a measure. Each section can be kept together with a plaiting band.

Plaiting a mane, and securing with needle and thread.

- Start at the poll and work down the neck. When plaiting, always ensure you pull the hair as tightly as possible and plait as far down the length of the mane as you can. If using a needle and thread then stitch round the bottom of the plait to ensure it does not come undone. Turn the plait under itself and under again. Bring the needle up through the middle of the plait, going left, under, back up and through, then the same to the right, then left, and right again. Then bring the needle down through the plait itself. Pull the thread taut and cut it off close to the plait.

Tail Plaiting

A tail plait is most frequently used when taking a horse showing and to other competition classes and his tail is not pulled. Horses taken hunting may also have their tails plaited. Plaiting the tail allows the hindquarters to be shown off to advantage and also tidies up the top of the tail.

The tail must first be washed and well brushed out. Make sure you have a plaiting band and needle and thread to hand. You must position yourself safely – do not corner yourself.

There are two methods of tail plaiting – a flat plait and a ridge plait. A ridge plait is more difficult and takes a great deal of practice to perfect. It does look impressive when complete though.

To plait a tail

- At the very top of the dock take a few hairs from either side of the tail and some from the centre. These may be tied with thread to give a firm start if you feel this will make the task easier when you are learning.

- These three strands form the plait. It is very important to keep the plaiting tight and close to the dock of the tail. If it becomes loose then it will be untidy and not stay plaited.

- Work down the tail, taking a few hairs from each side of the dock and bringing them into the middle to plait in. Make sure you take in only a few hairs at a time from the sides, or the plait will be too bulky.

- Ensure the centre of the plait is straight and down the middle of the tail.

- When you are about two-thirds of the way down the dock continue plaiting with just the hair you have and do not take any more from the sides. When you reach the end of this hair then stitch the end or secure it with a plaiting band.

- Loop the end up just under the main plait and secure it by sewing.

- For a flat plait the locks of hair are brought inwards and passed one over the top of the other. For a ridge plait the locks of hair are passed from underneath at the centre of the tail to make a ridge that stands up on top of the tail.

Plaiting a tail.

  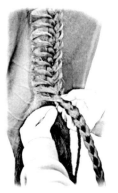 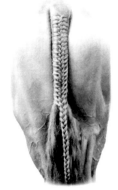

starting the plait   completing the end of the plait   looping under and stitching to secure   finished tail

What the assessor will look for

- You are likely to be asked to demonstrate your system of grooming a horse thoroughly. You may be asked to describe 'quartering', 'brushing off after work', 'full groom' and 'strapping'. Be sure that you can discuss fully the knowledge behind each of these terms, and that you are able to show a vigorous ability to groom the horse with the body brush and curry comb.

- You should not only demonstrate competence but show, through discussion, your understanding of safe practice, positioning yourself and/or the horse in such a way that injury is minimised when grooming the face, hind legs and picking up feet. For instance, you must not allow yourself to become cornered behind the horse's hind legs when grooming or plaiting. Always remember when grooming to stand in a position where you can observe what the hind legs are doing.

- Throughout your grooming work you should demonstrate an awareness of the horse's reaction and manner to you (e.g. you must recognise if he is ticklish in sensitive areas and threatens to nip or kick; similarly when banging you should be aware of the horse's acceptance of the activity).

- You should be aware of how much time it would be practical to allocate each horse if you were responsible for more than one. You should be able to estimate that it might take 5 minutes to quarter in the morning, 30 to 40 minutes for a full groom/strapping, and another 5 to 15 minutes to make the horse comfortable after work.

- Knowledge of how the after-work care might vary according to weather conditions (a wet or muddy horse) or how hard the horse has worked (washing off a sweaty horse) would be expected.

- Efficient use of time is essential if you are responsible for more than one horse and this also demonstrates your competence. If asked to groom, try to forget the assessor and 'get on with the job' as if you really had to turn the horse out immaculately for your employer.

- You are likely to be asked to put one or two plaits in a mane. This is most likely to be with a needle and thread, so make sure that you are proficient. If you are a little nervous, a fiddly job like plaiting can be difficult if you are not totally familiar with the task in normal circumstances. The mane may be too short/long/thick/thin. Be prepared to discuss the condition of the mane and how easy it is to manage.

- You may be asked to plait a tail. You must be able to do this. So if this is something you cannot yet do, ask someone to show you how and then practise thoroughly before your exam.

How to become competent

- In any establishment there are always horses who will benefit from a little extra time spent on grooming them.

- Unless there are several horses that you are responsible for on a daily basis, then you must go out of your way to practise grooming procedure and work on your system, efficiency and timing.

- Ask your instructor, or preferably someone who is a BHS assessor, to watch you groom and to ask you questions. Accept constructive criticism and work to be more proficient.

- Make sure that you are able to explain clearly the theory behind good grooming.

- Make sure that you can demonstrate and explain the following: quartering; brushing off after work; strapping; banging; grooming the face; grooming (finger-combing) the tail; sponging the eyes, nose and dock; plaiting a mane and tail in full (with thread).

- Get into the habit of doing these tasks without gloves on.

- Be fully aware of the reasons for the after-care of the horse when he has worked.

Clothing

The candidate should be able to:

Prepare a horse for travelling

Know:

Procedures for fitting and storing clothing and equipment

Rugs

By this stage, you should have come across a variety of rugs in your day-to-day care of horses over the seasons of the year. These should include rugs worn at night in the

A well-fitted outdoor/New Zealand rug, with gussets at the shoulder to allow for room and flexibility of movement.

Modern cooler rugs 'wick' away the sweat. If they don't have cross-over straps to secure them, you need a roller and withers pad. This horse is also tacked up for travelling.

A warm night rug with correctly fitted under-rug for extra warmth.

stable; rugs used for turnout; rugs used for fly protection; anti-sweat rugs and rugs for travelling in different weather conditions. You should be able to recognise lightweight rugs for summer and heavier ones for winter. You should have an understanding of the fact that using heavyweight rugs in summer can cause a horse stress and know that you can test a horse's body temperature by feeling the base of his ears. The more types of rugs you have encountered, the better. (*See The BHS Complete Training Manual for Stage 1* for notes on different types of rug, and rug-fitting.)

Bandages

Bandages are used for protection, warmth and support. Travel and stable bandages are similar. They are made of wool or man-made fibre and are 4 to 5 inches (10–13cm) wide and about 7 feet (2.13m) long. For both you use stable bandages that are not elasticised, with some form of padding under the bandage to provide warmth, protection and comfort for the horse. The two most popular forms of padding are Fybagee and Gamgee. Gamgee is cotton wool with thin gauze over it. Fybagee is a more substantial felt-like material that comes pre-cut to a 'leg size'. You can also purchase Fybagee pads that incorporate high knee and hock protection. The padding in a travel bandage is placed lower than that of a stable bandage so as to provide more protection for the coronary band and heel.

Elasticated bandages should not be used for travel or stable bandages. They may well become too tight and cause ligament or circulatory issues. Elasticated bandages are used for exercise work and are assessed in Stage 3.

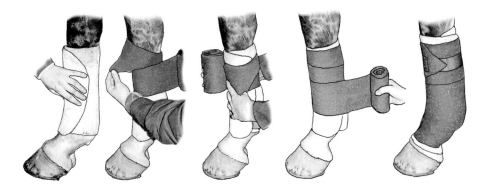

Sequence for putting on a bandage.

Bandaging.

Stable bandage – padding just below the bandage, to prevent unnecessary interference with bedding

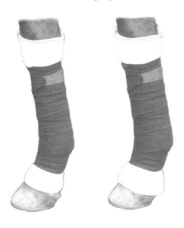

Travel bandage – more padding for protection, and padding lower to protect coronary band

Putting on a stable or travel bandage

- Make sure the leg is clean and dry.

- Wrap Fybagee/Gamgee round the leg, going from the front of the leg to the back.

- Place the bandage against the leg, ensuring that the bandage will be put on from the front to the back of the leg (i.e. on the nearside legs of the horse, bandage in an anticlockwise direction; and on the offside legs, bandage in a clockwise direction). The padding must always be wrapped in the same direction.

- Start near the top of the cannon bone, just below the knee, and, after having gone round the leg once, the end of the bandage can be turned down and bandaged over to help with security.

- Bandage down the leg, overlapping the bandage halfway each time, ensuring the tension is even and the bandage has no wrinkles. Bandage over the fetlock and down the pastern, keeping the tension and overlap the same. (This requires a lot of practice.)

- Slightly angle the last turn at the bottom of the foot down and then angle up the first turn up the pastern. This will give you a V shape in the middle of the pastern at the front.

- Bandage back up the leg with the same overlap and tension. Hopefully you will be able to fasten the tapes or secure the Velcro tab at the outer side of the horse's leg.

- Make sure the fastening is no tighter than the bandage itself. If the bandage has tapes, tie them in a bow and tuck the ends under the rest of the tape. You can then pull the last loop of bandage down over them to help prevent them from coming undone and to make it all look tidier.

- To test the tension, place a finger down inside the padding. You should be able to fit a single finger snugly. If it is too tight the circulation in the leg will be impaired and this can lead to tendon and (in extreme cases) foot damage. If the bandage is too loose it may come undone or slip down the horse's leg, causing the horse to trip and the bandage to break.

Removing a stable or travel bandage

- To remove a leg bandage, first undo the fastenings and then quickly and efficiently unwrap the bandage from the leg, collecting it in your hands. Do not try to roll up the bandage as you are taking it off. This can be a very slow process and you will not get the bandage rolled up taut enough to put back on correctly. Take the padding off and then massage down the back of the horse's leg to encourage circulation. Then re-roll the bandage ready for re use.

Preparing a horse for travelling

When tacking up a horse for travelling, first check the size of your horse and then collect suitable size equipment. You need to consider the following:

- headcollar

- poll guard

- rug

- tail bandage

- tail guard

- leg protection (either travel boots, or bandages and knee boots, and possibly over-reach boots

You need to take the weather conditions into consideration. If it is a cold day then a

Horse dressed to travel, with poll guard, rug appropriate to weather conditions, tail bandage and tail guard, and travelling boots for leg protection.

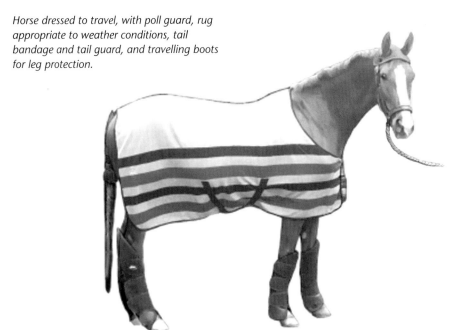

thick cooler rug may be the best option. A smart woollen day rug may also be a possibility. If it is warm then a summer sheet or thin cooler may be ideal; and if it is very hot you may feel that travelling without a rug may be the best thing.

You should travel a horse in a leather headcollar if at all possible. A leather headcollar will break in an emergency whereas a nylon one will not. A poll guard should be attached to the headcollar. There are various types of poll guard. One type fits over the horse's ears as well as through the headpiece of the headcollar. When fitting this type be aware that the horse may find it a little strange if he is not used to it. The second type has a thick piece of sponge on slots that permit attachment to the headpiece of the headcollar. Whatever the type it is easier to fit the poll guard to the headcollar first and then put both on together. With the design that fits over the ears it is worthwhile putting it on the horse before fitting it to the headcollar so he has had the feeling of it.

In the exam you may well be asked to fit travel bandages and knee boots in front, and travel boots behind. (You will not be asked to fit hock boots.) Put on your travel bandage first as previously described, and then put the knee boot on.

The top strap of the knee boot should fit above the knee and be fastened tightly enough so that it will not slip down over the knee. The bottom strap of the knee boot should be loose. This is attached solely to stop the boot flipping up, and if it is too tight it can impede the horse's movement. This should be fitted over the travel bandage.

There are many designs of travel boot. They should be long enough to protect both the knee/hock and the coronary band. If they are not long enough then overreach boots may need to be fitted. Make sure you look at the boots carefully and fit them to the correct leg and the correct way up. The Velcro fittings should always do up from front to back and be on the outside of the leg. The boot should be pulled taut as the Velcro is done up so that it does not fall down or come undone in transit.

You also need to fit a tail bandage. Some people also put on a tail guard for extra protection. Again there are various types of tail guard. Some have long tapes that are designed to fix round a roller. Remember if you fit a roller you must have a withers pad. The tapes should not be so tight that they lift the horse's tail. You should be able to get a vertical flat hand between the tapes and the horse's back.

It is more aesthetically pleasing if all the travel equipment matches and is neat and tidy.

Rug storage

Before rugs are stored for the summer they should be cleaned, and repaired if necessary. Synthetic rugs can be washed in a washing machine. New Zealand rugs will usually need to be re-waterproofed. There are many specialist companies that can do this. Some will take a dirty rug and clean it as well; others prefer you to have scrubbed the rug clean first. Once the rugs have been cleaned and repaired any leather fastenings should be oiled. The rugs can then be folded and stored away in a dry bin or trunk that is moth-free. Rugs must be dry before storing away, and the place where they are stored must be dry to avoid mould forming.

What the assessor is looking for

- The assessor will expect you to be able to identify a range of rugs and may want to test your ability to choose the rug, or rugs, which are most appropriate to the weather conditions of the day or the conditions in which a horse might have to travel (e.g. lorry or trailer).

- When handling horses that you know well, it is easy to become complacent about how you manage them. It is, however, essential when dealing with an unfamiliar or young horse, that you adopt a procedure for fitting equipment that is safe for both you and the horse, in the event that he behaves unpredictably. Whereas at home, with your own horse, it would be quite acceptable to throw a rug over his back, this would not be wise with a horse that is unfamiliar to you. The assessor will expect you to demonstrate a procedure for applying rugs to a horse that is unfamiliar to you (even if you are taking the exam at a centre where you know the horses well). With this in mind, fold rugs and blankets and place them a little way up the neck, then unfold them over the horse's back.

- Throughout the fitting of horse clothing you will be expected to discuss whether the item does or does not fit the horse. If the fit is inappropriate you need to discuss clearly the reasons why. Check the length of the rug over the back and ensure it protects the top of the dock. Check the depth of rug – it should not look like a mini skirt! Look at the shoulders and make sure the rug does not appear to be stretched tight over them. This could lead to bare patches of coat at the horse's point of shoulder. Always make sure the rug does not put pressure onto the crest just above the withers. This usually happens when the front is too small and makes everything too tight when the buckles are done up. Rugs are usually measured from the point of shoulder to the point of buttock and are sold in 3-inch incremental sizes. This element of the exam is often assessed within the tacking up for travel section when a suitable rug for travelling the horse for that day is fitted with the rest of the travel tack.

- Be familiar with the fitting of bandages for travel and for wear in the stable. Be able to discuss types of bandage materials used and the types of padding or protection that might be used underneath the bandages. Be able to talk about the different jobs that each type of bandage is employed to do for the horse (e.g. stable bandages for warmth, travel bandages for protection).

- You will be asked to demonstrate the application of a travel bandage.

- You will have to tack up a horse for travelling. You may well be asked to dress a horse for 'a 50-mile journey today'. Your choice of rug (or even whether the horse should wear one) will depend on the weather. As long as you can justify your choice, there should be no problem.

Assessors are often presented with horses tacked up for travel wearing travelling boots that are upside down. This shows a lack of practical knowledge. Make sure the Velcro is done up from front to back on the horse's leg and the shape of the boot follows the contours of the horse's leg. Sometimes there are other clues to guide you – for example a Woof boot has a W on it, so make sure this the right way up, showing a W not an M.

- Throughout the fitting of all the clothing you must demonstrate a safe procedure for both your own and the horse's welfare. You must be sufficiently competent at the tasks to show a relevant speed for completion appropriate to the level (i.e. someone at Stage 2 level would be quicker and more efficient than someone of Stage 1 ability).

- You may be asked about conditions for storing and caring for rugs and clothing in general.

- You should know that equipment and clothing that does not fit properly is a potential danger to the horse and the equipment.

How to become competent

- Handle horses in as many different types of yard as you can. In this way you are likely to see horses wearing a variety of rugs for different weathers and appropriate to different after-work conditions.

- Make sure that you regularly apply rugs and remove them following a safe and efficient system. (You may throw rugs onto a familiar horse, but practise until you are completely competent at folding rugs and applying them as if to a nervous or unknown horse.)

- Ask your instructor to supervise and monitor regularly your application of rugs and bandages. Practise with Fybagee and Gamgee as they feel very different to work with.

- By working around horses in different weather conditions and seeing horses travel to competitions you will develop an awareness of which type of rug to choose for any situation.

- If a horse in your yard needs to wear stable bandages or is travelling regularly, ask if you can put on his equipment. If this is not possible then find the equipment and practise with it often so that you are familiar and efficient with the task. Remember that in an exam you may be nervous, which can lower your proficiency.

- Observe other, more experienced people applying rugs and bandages. It can be very motivating to watch someone who is quick and efficient. Your aim should be to emulate their competence.

- If you are not responsible for keeping rugs and equipment in good condition then ask your instructor about washing and re-proofing. Most rugs today are machine washable, but if they are outdoor rugs they may have to be re-proofed. Your local saddler can also advise about this.

UNIT 1b

Fit, Remove and Maintain Tack for Exercise

3 Credits

Saddlery

Fit and remove tack for exercise

Select, use and maintain tack and work safely

Know:

How to fit tack and remove for exercise

The cleaning and care of all saddlery

Ill-fitting tack

Ill-fitting tack of any sort will be uncomfortable for the horse. This can lead to rubbing, galls and sore patches. A horse may well become fretful and difficult to tack up or he may not be able to be ridden. Once a rider is mounted the horse may try to run away from, or get rid of the pain. This can lead to the rider falling off, causing injury and loss of confidence.

Checking the fit of a bridle

When checking the fit of a bridle, look at the following:

- Check that the bit is not too low or too high in the horse's mouth. The bit should make the corner of the horse's lips 'smile' with one or two wrinkles visible.

- The bit should not be too small nor too large for the horse's mouth. To check the bit is the correct length for the horse's mouth, pull it through the mouth to one

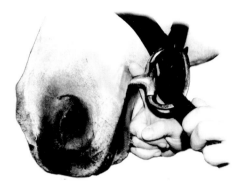

Checking that the width of the bit is the correct size for the horse.

side as far as you can and you should be able to get a finger between the ring of the bit and the mouth.

- The bit should not have any worn areas as these could pinch the lips or tongue. If you come across an old looking bit made of nickel (a yellowy coloured metal as opposed to the more common silver-coloured stainless steel) you need to check it for wear very carefully. There are not many nickel bits in use nowadays, but there are still some around. It is generally easy to distinguish between a nickel bit and the modern bits made of copper-based materials. The newer bits are generally thicker, do not look worn and are often of an up-to-date design. Some of these are stamped with the maker's initials.

- The bit should not be too thick for the horse's mouth. Some rubber and vulcanite bits are very thick, and a horse with a small mouth and a big tongue may find such bits uncomfortable in his mouth.

- The noseband should be between one and two finger-widths below the protruding cheek bone so that it does not rub the bone. A cavesson noseband should be done up as tightly as is the policy for the riding centre. Some centres use a cavesson noseband purely for aesthetic reasons and others use one to help keep a horse's mouth closed. It is felt by some that it is unfair to use a cavesson noseband in this way as they believe a very tight noseband causes the horse great pain. If fitting a noseband with a flash strap the cavesson part of the noseband should be at the same height as a simple cavesson noseband. This should be done up tightly enough so that when the flash strap is done up it does not pull the cavesson down. The buckle of a flash strap should not be done up near the horse's lips and the bit. This can cause rubbing and soreness. The buckle should be either on the nose or in the curb groove.

- The browband of the bridle should not be so tight that it pulls the head piece forward onto the ears, or that it rubs the forehead of the horse. Check also that it is not too big. This can cause it to move up and down as the horse moves, which could annoy him.

- The throatlash should be done up so that the horse is able to flex at the poll and not be impeded by it being too tight. Traditionally you should be able to get a flat hand between the throatlash and the cheek bone. There are some new designs of bridle that do not have throatlashes. These tend to be used for dressage.

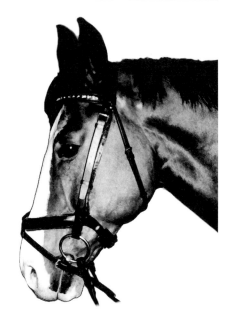

An incorrectly fitted flash noseband. The flash strap is pulling the cavesson down and is buckled on the horse's lip.

- The leather of the bridle should not be too thick or too thin for the horse's face. A heavyweight cob will look rather silly in a thin leather bridle that is designed for a chisel-faced pony or Thoroughbred, and vice versa. The leather should all be in good condition. Old tack is fine as long as it is well maintained, supple and the stitching is in good order.

- Reins should be in good condition and, if there is a running martingale, they should have rubber stops on them.

- Remember that buckle fastenings are always on the outside of a bridle and billet fastenings turn in towards the horse's skin.

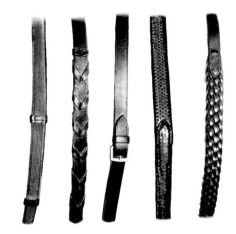

Reins come in a variety of materials to provide a different feel or additional grip. L to Rt: continental, laced, plain, rubber, plaited.

- Hold the bridle up by the horse's head to get an approximate fit before trying to actually fit it on the horse. (How to put the bridle on a horse is covered in the Stage 1 book.)

- When fitting a bridle always pull the cheekpiece and noseband ends out of the keepers so you can quickly and efficiently alter the position of the bit and noseband if it is not correct.

- After you have fitted the bridle, ensuring that everything is level, put the leather back in the keepers, twist the reins up, putting one rein through the throat lash, and put the headcollar back on over the bridle.

Checking a bridle for approximate fit before applying it.

Checking the fit of the saddle

When assessing the fit of a saddle it is not expected that a Stage 2 candidate replaces a qualified saddle fitter. It is a basic understanding that is required so that a badly fitting saddle will be easily spotted thus ensuring that a horse will not be in any pain.

The following are important points to recognise and understand:

- The saddle must be in the correct place on the horse's back. This should be the lowest point on his back. This is found by placing the saddle forward on his withers and sliding it back by pushing down and back on the pommel so that the saddle slides back as far as it will comfortably go.

- The saddle size should appear the correct size for the horse i.e. not overly small or large for his build. The saddle should not sit any further back than the last thoracic vertebra. If it does there is a danger of placing excess weight on the loins, which can injure the horse.

45

General-purpose saddle fitted with numnah and breastplate.

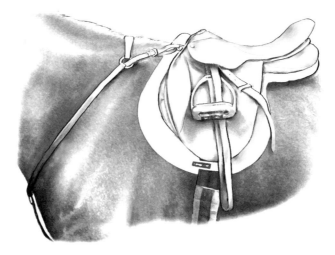

- The width of the saddle should ensure that it is not too narrow to cause pinching at the withers or down the spine. It must not be too wide either, or this can mean that the saddle moves around too much, which will cause rubbing and soreness. It can also cause the saddle to be too low on the horse's withers.

- There must be clear daylight down the gullet along the horse's back when a rider is mounted. Some people say it is necessary to have three to four fingers clearance between the pommel and the spine before the rider is mounted to achieve this. This does, however, depend on the design of the saddle.

- The gullet must be wide enough to ensure it does not press on any part of the horse's spine.

- The panels of the saddle should all be in contact with the horse to ensure even weight distribution. Make sure the panels under the seat of the saddle are in maximum contact with horse's back and not just sitting on the back at one point. Running your fingers down between the panel and the horse's skin at the front of the saddle will help you to feel if the saddle is too narrow and pinching. If there is no contact then the saddle could move too much, rub and cause friction.

- The length of the flaps must suit both the horse and the rider. The rider's lower leg should not be impeded in any way by the length of the flap.

- Always fit a saddle without a numnah first to ensure a correct fit.

Saddle safety

- Never leave a saddle unattended on a horse without the girth done up.

- Never leave a saddle on the door of a stable when the horse is not tied up as he is likely to knock it to the ground with the potential for damage.

Different types of saddle.

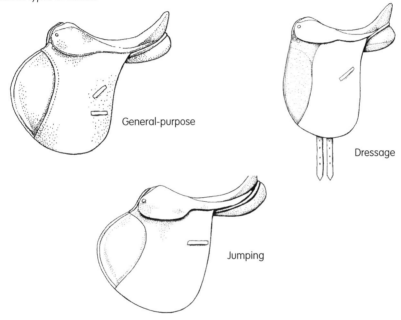

General-purpose

Dressage

Jumping

- Look at the way the saddle sits on the horse. The cantle should not be lower than the pommel. If it is it will push the rider's weight back towards the horse's loins, which will be uncomfortable for both horse and rider.

- The girth straps should always have a buckle guard and this should be pulled down over the girth buckles to help protect the saddle flap from wear and tear. Ideally the girth should do up about halfway on either side of the saddle when secured for riding.

- The stirrup irons should have stirrup treads and the stirrup leathers should be well oiled, not worn, thin or cracked, and with the stitching secure.

- A saddle is measured from the stud below the pommel to the middle of the cantle. They usually come in half-inch sizes. A 17-inch saddle is the most usual size for the 'average' horse and rider.

Fitting a breastplate or martingale

- When fitting a breastplate and/or martingale, ensure that you can get a flat hand's width between all the points where the leather is close to the horse.

- Carefully inspect the loop between the horse's legs where it attaches to the girth. This leather should not be so long that there is the potential for a cantering horse to catch it with his feet. The same applies to the size of the loop round the girth.

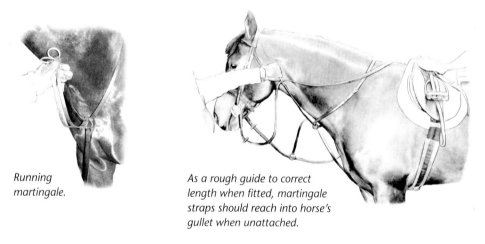

Running martingale.

As a rough guide to correct length when fitted, martingale straps should reach into horse's gullet when unattached.

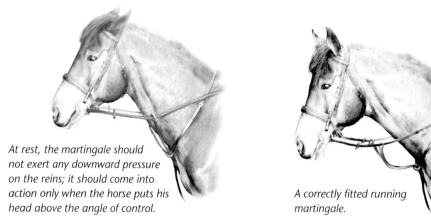

At rest, the martingale should not exert any downward pressure on the reins; it should come into action only when the horse puts his head above the angle of control.

A correctly fitted running martingale.

A leather Atherstone girth with elasticated end.

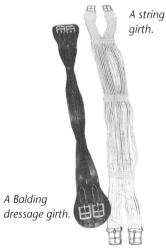

A string girth.

A fabric girth. There are many different brand names.

A Balding dressage girth.

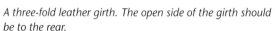

A three-fold leather girth. The open side of the girth should be to the rear.

- If there are two points of attachment on the saddle for the breastplate, always use the more secure one, which is under the skirt and attached directly through to the tree.

- The neckstrap buckle should be on the nearside of the horse.

- A running martingale should be fitted as per the illustration on page 48. Make sure there are stops on the reins and a rubber martingale stop holding the neckstrap and martingale strap together.

Tacking up a horse for exercise

An efficient way to undertake this task is as follows:

- Put a headcollar on the horse, tie him up and skip him out.

- While doing this assess his general size and shape so you choose tack that is liable to fit.

- Collect all the equipment you need: saddle, numnah, bridle, breastplate/ martingale, boots. Place the equipment tidily outside the box.

- Fit the bridle as discussed on pages 42–45. Put the headcollar on over the bridle, having twisted the reins and put one of them up through the throatlash.

- Depending on the weather and the horse's coat, take the horse's rug off, or fold it back, leaving the loins warm.

- Fit the saddle without the numnah – if you are quick and efficient at this and do not leave the horse alone you do not need to attach the girth. Remove the saddle.

- Put on the breastplate/martingale.

- Put the numnah under the saddle; take the girth with you and fit and secure the saddle, remembering to thread the loop of the breastplate/martingale through the girth having first checked the fit. Make sure the numnah is pulled well up into the gullet and ensure it is attached to the saddle as per the fastenings of that particular numnah.

- Attach the breastplate to the D-rings at the pommel. If there are two rings to choose from, use the one that is attached directly to the tree under the skirt. This is safer than the one at the front edge of the saddle which is attached by a small piece of leather. This could easily break.

- Make sure you can get an upturned flat hand comfortably under the attachment strap.

- If the breastplate has a martingale attachment, untwist the reins and attach the martingale, making sure the rings run smoothly along the reins. Check there are martingale stops on the reins.

- If the weather is cold, place the rug back over the saddle to help keep the horse warm.

- Put on the boots you have selected.

Leg protection/support (boots)

Boots are designed to offer support and/or protection. There are numerous different designs and manufacturers of boots for protection when a horse is working.

- **Brushing boots** fit around the cannon bone and are shaped to protect the fetlock as well. The front boots usually have two, three or four straps, and the hind boots four or five. The straps should do up from front to back, and the straps should be tight enough to prevent the boot slipping down, but not so tight that they interfere with the blood supply.

- When fitting a boot, wrap it around the leg a little higher than required. If the middle strap is done up first, it helps to keep the boot in position. Then do up the upper strap, and work down so that the bottom strap is the last to be fastened. Push the boot down into place and check with your fingers that the whole of the fetlock is protected. Test that the boot is tight enough by ensuring you can fit a finger snugly between the leg and the top of the boot.

Brushing boot with over-reach boot.

- There are some brushing boots that have double Velcro on them. With these, usually the inner part does up from front to back, and the outer part from back to front. Whatever the boot, check the shape and make sure you fit it to the shape of the leg.

- **Tendon boots** are usually open-fronted, with the back of the boot padded to protect the tendons. They are frequently used when show jumping. They are fitted in the same way as brushing boots.

- **Over-reach boots** protect the coronet and heel. There are several types, principally in two groups: one that does up with some form of buckle; and one that has to be turned inside out, pulled up over the foot and then turned down to rest on the leg above the coronet and over the foot.

Open-fronted tendon boot.

What the assessor is looking for

- You must be able to recognise ill-fitting tack, and tack which is not appropriate to the horse, for whatever reason. Examples would be: a pinching browband or one which is too small; a noseband which is rubbing against a cheek bone, or a bit which is incorrectly fitted, causing friction in the mouth. Inappropriate tack might include saddlery in need of repair and numnahs or girths that need washing.

- You must understand and be able to describe the consequences of using ill-fitting tack. These include the risk of injury and discomfort to the horse, both of which may result in an accident to the rider.

- You will be required to fit tack for everyday use. Your tack fitting must be efficient and workmanlike. It must have due regard for the safety of the horse and the equipment.

- Your tack fitting must be systematic and thorough, so that it leaves the horse safely equipped for the rider. For example, when fitting the bridle, check the fit of browband, the fit of throatlash, the position and tightness of the noseband, and the position and width of the bit.

- You will be expected to choose and apply some boots which might be used for everyday use.

- You will be asked to put on some type of breastplate and/or a martingale. The martingale will either be a running or standing type, so be familiar with both.

- You will be asked to talk about the maintenance of tack, including everyday care and the seasonal treatment of rugs and other equipment, which needs to be safely stored for the winter or summer off-season. See also page 37.

How to become competent

- Try to apply tack to horses that you are less familiar with, and handle the tack with a more inquisitive approach. Look at the condition of the leather and consider its maintenance – do you think it is supple and well cared for?

- From time to time try to fit tack to horses using items that will not automatically fit. Undo all the keepers and practise measuring the bridle against the horse's head to estimate fit. Remember, once you are happy with the fit, then replace all the keepers so that the bridle is fitted neatly and tidily.

- Learn to look at saddles with a view to judging whether the saddle looks too big or too small on the horse's back. Your common sense will tell you if the saddle looks as if it swamps the horse, or if it looks like a 'pea on a drum'.

- Ask your instructor to show you clearly how to assess saddle fit, including the clearance over the withers, the fit on the shoulders, the room along the spine, and the length and depth of the saddle.

- Whenever you see other horses (not those you know), look at the type of boots they are wearing and consider the type of work they might be doing in those particular boots. (At a show jumping competition, for example, you may see a lot of open-fronted tendon boots, whereas at a dressage show you will see far more brushing/schooling boots, usually white.)

- Look in your local tack shops at the wide variety of boots now available. Most boots will say on them what specific job they are designed for.

- Make sure that you have fitted boots as often as possible.

- The more experience you have of applying various types of boots and saddlery, the easier it will be in your exam when there is a wide range of equipment available and you must choose items to fit to a specific horse.

- Make sure that you have had lots of practice in the day-to-day care and cleaning of tack, so that you can easily recognise tack in supple and good condition and that which is dry, hard and neglected.

- Try to have used a range of cleaning products, such as bar saddle soap, neatsfoot oil and heavy-duty leather dressing.

- Be aware of how you maintain tack that is thoroughly wet and muddy, new tack, and neglected dry tack.

- Notice how boots are cleaned and maintained in your yard. Get involved in this procedure, even if you are not a full-time worker in the establishment.

- Whenever you get the opportunity, discuss the tack that is used at your establishment: find out what is used, when and why. Watch others who are more experienced than you fit equipment. Ask questions about anything you have not seen or experienced before.

- Hands-on practice and observation of others using various pieces of equipment builds competence.

Handling

Safety

When looking after horses it is vital that your personal safety as well as that of the horses and the equipment you are using are taken into consideration. There is a myth that there is a 'BHS way' of doing everything and if you do not undertake tasks in that way you will not pass your exams. This is not true – there are ways to undertake tasks that are safe for you, your horse and the equipment and, as long as the methods you use fulfil these criteria, then you will pass.

Horses are big, heavy, nervous creatures that may be unpredictable. With confident, consistent handling they often become quieter, but there may always be the potential for volatile behaviour. If you are a horse owner you and your horse may be used to certain routines for tasks and you may take some liberties in the way in which you undertake these jobs. For instance you may throw your rugs up and over your horse and he will be used to this and will not be frightened. If, however, you throw rugs up onto a strange horse he may not be used to this and react strongly to the action. By ensuring a few simple rules you can reduce the possibility of accidents happening.

- Always talk to a horse before approaching him.

- Always tie a horse up with a quick-release knot when working in the stable or grooming.

- Wear the correct clothing necessary to protect yourself for the tasks you are undertaking.

- Be confident but calm around horses.

- Always remain alert, watching the horse's body language.

- Do not get yourself trapped in the corner of a stable.

- Do not stand behind a horse.

- Keep the yard and equipment tidy.

- Always lead an unknown horse in a bridle.

- Use your common sense.

The list could go on and on, but being confident, observant, sensible, thoughtful and consistent are the most important factors. When working in an exam always work around the horses as if you do not know them, even if you do.

Accidents do happen when working around horses, but if you work within the above parameters you can keep these to a minimum.

What the assessor is looking for

- Anyone involved in any aspect of riding or caring for horses should recognise that the very nature of the activity conveys a degree of risk. This is not only because the horse is an animal but also because he is a big animal, which, mismanaged or handled badly, could cause injury.

- Anyone working in and around horses will identify a wide range of 'risks' in the stable yard and while riding. The most valuable asset that you can develop is awareness around the stable yard, particularly in the vicinity of any horse, but especially around those with whom you are unfamiliar.

- You must be able to describe or list some of the risks, minor and major, to you and the horse in and around stables. These would include dangers such as being trodden on by a horse, a horse tripping over equipment left in the yard (wheelbarrow or fork) and injuring himself, a rope burn from a horse pulling away from you if not wearing gloves – the list is endless!

- You must demonstrate procedures which safeguard you and the horse in every situation. For example, a safe procedure for mucking out a horse would be:

    - tie the horse up (or remove him if it is practical to do so);

    - gather all necessary equipment and keep it tidily outside the stable door;

    - keep the equipment outside the stable unless you are actually using it;

• stay aware of the horse and his reactions at all times;

• on completing the task, untie the horse and safely bolt the stable door, removing all equipment to its appropriate and original place.

• The safety element, whether for the protection of yourself or the horse, of every procedure that you use must be clearly evident – e.g. the wearing of gloves when turning a horse out safeguards against the risk of a horse pulling away from you and giving you a rope burn on unprotected hands. Wearing a hat for the same task helps to protect your head from knocks and kicks.

• The methods you adopt in handling horses must demonstrate practical

Mucking out in a safe environment. Horse tied up and all equipment that is not in use is safely outside the door.

competence, and where necessary would show that you were able to give confidence to a horse whilst still maintaining control. For example, if a horse is being strong and unruly, it may be necessary to wrap the lead rope through the noseband of the headcollar and over his nose to give added control; it may be necessary to put a bridle on him; and in extreme cases use a device such as a Chifney to insist on obedience. Your knowledge and competence must be evident in this respect, but also your ability to soothe and reward the horse when he is brought under control and is obedient.

- Efficient use of time will be required on all occasions throughout this and other levels of competence. Quite simply, efficient use of time in any aspect of practical work demonstrates your familiarity with the task through frequent practice. 'Good practice makes perfect' may be a well-worn saying but it is nevertheless appropriate. The only way you will develop efficiency in using your time is through plenty of practical application.

- It is essential that you keep all your equipment safe and tidy. This is important to ensure that the equipment is not damaged or lost and gives a professional air to your work.

- As per any formal occasion you should make sure you are dressed appropriately. Shirts should be tucked in and ties done up correctly with a traditional knot at the throat, covering the top button of the shirt. Boots must be clean for the start of the day. Although you must be tidily dressed you should also be at ease so that you can work efficiently without feeling uncomfortable.

  A clean and tidy sweatshirt and/or waistcoat is suitable for all sections of the exam. Make sure you have enough clothes if the weather is cold. A change of clothes may be useful if the weather is wet. If it is a warm day you may ride without your jacket as long as your arms are covered.

  Do read the guidelines for dress, which are available from the Examinations Office at the BHS.

How to become competent

- The more you work in the stable yard and the more practice you have in handling stabled horses and those kept at grass, the better.

- Discuss with your yard manager or your instructor the areas covered by the Health and Safety policy of the establishment and also the risk assessment procedure.

- If you are a full-time student then these areas should have already been introduced to you. The yard should have certain procedures in place which are there for your safety and that of the horses. Make sure that you follow these policies, and if you are not sure why they are there, then ask.

- Inevitably you will learn by experience (we all do). It is hoped that the experiences you have will not be too painful nor in any way inhibiting. For example, no one who has worked for any length of time with horses can say they have never been trodden on; however, once you have been trodden on (and it does hurt) then you are much more careful about your proximity to the horse's feet and you realise why sturdy shoes or boots are important.

- Break down all the tasks and activities that you do with horses and think of all the areas of risk that are involved with those tasks. If you do this task by task (with some help from your instructor if not a full-time student) then you will build up a comprehensive list of the areas where your awareness needs to be strong and increased. For example, in icy weather the yard is likely to be more slippery. Therefore be careful to pour water carefully into drains; do not allow water to spill – and freeze – on the yard; sprinkle salt or sand on the yard to reduce slip; wear ridged soled shoes to assist in grip; lead horses with added care.

UNIT 2a

The Principles of Horse Health and Anatomy

8 Credits

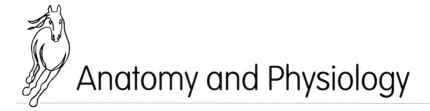

Anatomy and Physiology

The candidate should know:

The horse's skeleton

The structure, function and potential problems of the horse's foot

The position of the main internal organs

The basic structure of the horse's digestive system

How to recognise a horse's health, welfare and condition

How to recognise and treat minor wounds

How to care for sick horses

The importance of keeping horse records

The importance of worming

The skeleton

For Stage 2 you must know the horse's skeletal structure and be confident enough to point to the different bones on the horse that is in the stable with you. A common mistake that candidates make is to point to the cervical vertebrae as if they follow the line of the horse's crest rather than down through the middle of the neck. It is also important to know how many of each type of vertebrae the horse has.

The horse's skeleton has approximately 205 bones. These are split into the axial and appendicular skeletons. The axial skeleton consists of the skull, the spine, the sternum and ribs. The appendicular skeleton is formed by the fore and hind limbs.

The skeleton.

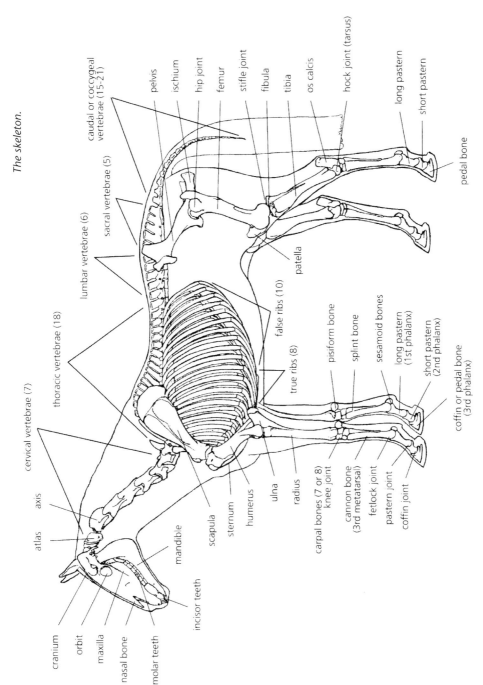

The axial skeleton.

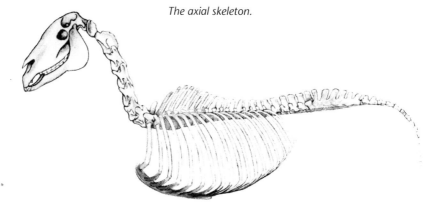

The appendicular skeleton.

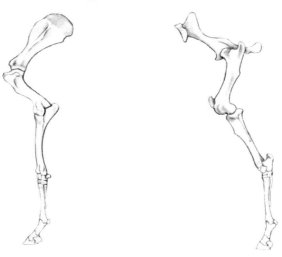

The horse has 18 pairs of ribs; each pair is fixed to one of the thoracic vertebrae. There are 8 pairs of true ribs and 10 pairs of false ribs. The true ribs are attached to the sternum, and the false ribs are attached by cartilage at their ends.

The foot

The old saying: 'No foot, no horse' is very true.

You must know the external and internal parts of the foot.

There are two and a half bones in the foot: the pedal bone, the navicular bone and half the short pastern bone.

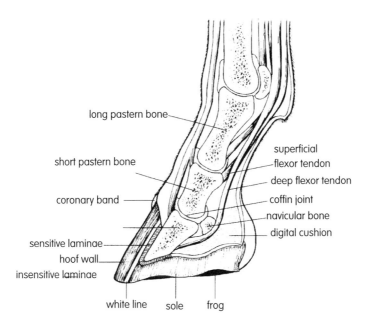

The foot and pastern. The bones of the lower leg, below the knee/hock, are identical in the front and hind limbs.

A horse's front feet are round in shape so that they can spread bodyweight over a greater area as they come in contact with the ground. The hind feet are more oval in shape. This is a more economical shape for pushing, which is the primary function of the hindquarters and legs.

The frog has a tough, elastic consistency and several functions:

- Each time it is pushed onto the ground, with the expansion of the foot, it helps pump blood and lymphatic fluid back up the legs.

- It helps to absorb the concussion created each time the foot touches the ground. This cuts down the amount of jarring that goes up the legs.

- It provides grip. Its triangular shape, with the cleft in the middle and the lateral clefts, help to make a firm footfall.

- It acts as a weight-bearing surface to help support the horse's weight.

The sole of the foot.

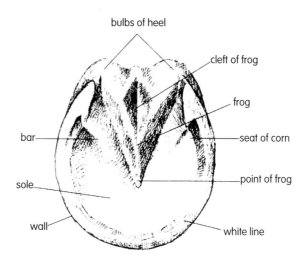

The white line forms the junction between the wall and the sole. This is an important guide for the farrier. On the inner side of the white line are the sensitive laminae, and if these are breached by a farrier's nail, the horse will, in all probability, be lame. Thus the nails have to go to the outside of the white line, through the insensitive horn, so their insertion does not cause pain.

- If a horse's feet are allowed to grow too long the hoof/pastern axis is broken. This could lead to tendon strain, bruising, heel pain, coffin joint inflammation and possibly navicular syndrome.

The main internal organs

It is important to know where the main internal organs of the horse are located. For instance, if you understand that the kidneys are positioned near to the horse's back, behind where a well-fitted saddle lies, you will be more aware of how a saddle that is too long can injure a horse and how important is is to keep this area (the loins) warm on a cold day.

Major internal organs of the horse. Note that the lungs (not shown) lie within the ribcage.

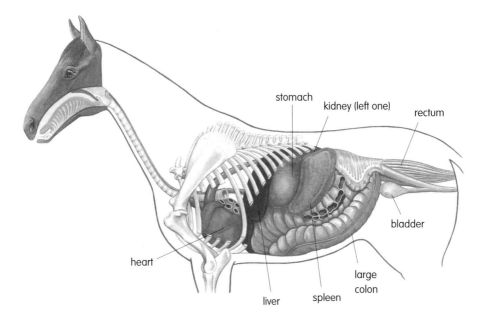

The digestive system

The horse's digestive system is complex and liable to problems. Having a basic understanding of how it works will assist the groom in ensuring the system works correctly and the horse stays healthy.

The term 'alimentary canal' refers to the whole system, from the lips to the anus.

The digestive system operates as follows:

- The muzzle feels for and separates food.

- The lips gather in the food.

- The incisor (front) teeth bite the food.

- The tongue is a large muscle that pushes the food back to the molar teeth. As in humans the tongue has a huge number of taste buds over its top surface.

- The molars masticate (chew and grind) the food. The food is mixed with saliva

The digestive system, simplified.

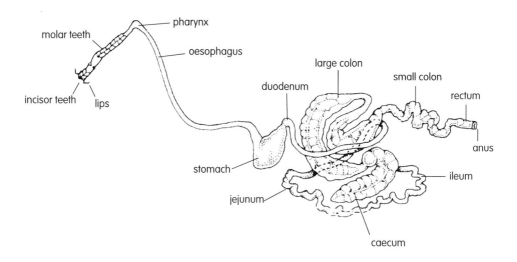

and as it is passed back to the pharynx (throat) it is formed into a bolus (a ball shape).

- The bolus travels over the epiglottis (which stops food moving down the trachea into the lungs) and into the oesophagus (gullet).

- The food travels down the oesophagus by peristalsis, a wave-like movement that pushes the food along. The bolus can be seen travelling down the gullet when the horse is eating.

- The bolus of food travels through the cardiac sphincter muscle into the stomach. This muscle acts as a 'non-return' valve. The disadvantage of this is that the horse cannot be sick. This means that potentially poisonous food cannot be ejected and has to travel all the way through the horse's system.

- The horse's stomach is very small for the size of his body. It is approximately the size of a rugby ball. This is one of the reasons why the horse is a 'trickle feeder' and cannot consume large amounts of food at any one time. Food can stay in the stomach for anything from thirty minutes to three hours. The stomach is mostly a holding vat for the rest of the system, although food breakdown does start here.

- The food then passes out of the stomach via the pyloric sphincter muscle and into the small intestine.

- The small intestine consists of the duodenum, the jejunum and the ileum. This is where the enzymes really start to break down the food.

- The partially broken down food then moves into the large intestine which consists of the caecum, large colon, small colon, rectum and anus. The large intestine continues the breakdown of the food and it is here that cellulose is broken down and digested. The bacteria in the gut perform this function. Each type of bacteria breaks down a certain type of food. That is why you must always change a horse's diet gradually. Put simply, if a horse is used to having a diet of barley and sugar-beet shreds for his hard food, he will have more bacteria in his gut that are designed specifically to break down these feed types. If you suddenly change him onto oats there will not be enough 'oat' bacteria to break down a large amount, and this could lead to digestive disorders like colic.

- Waste matter passes from the small colon into the rectum, forms into balls of dung and these are then passed out through the anus.

Without bulk the horse's digestive system will not continue to work. Bulk is the 'petrol' that keeps the engine going.

Health and condition

It is very important to be able to tell when a horse is in good health and when he is not. When looking after horses on a regular basis a groom gets to know a horse's normal behaviour and should be able to notice very quickly when he is 'off colour'. Knowing a horse's normal temperature, pulse and respiration rates (TPR) is an important indicator.

A horse's normal **TPR** rates are :

Temperature:	**38 °C/100.5 °F**
Pulse (at rest):	**36 to 42 beats per minute**
Respiration (at rest):	**8 to 12 breaths per minute**

Some signs of good health are as follows:

- Eating and drinking normally.

- Coat shiny with loose skin.

- Eyes bright and alert.

- Generally alert and interested in everything.

- Droppings normal and normal amount. (Droppings should break when they hit the ground. They are passed regularly throughout the day. The colour of droppings depends on the food the horse is eating.)

- Salmon-pink mucous membranes.

- Urine should be colourless or pale yellow and passed several times a day.

- Cool legs.

- No discharge from the eyes or nose.

- Standing on all four feet. A hind leg may be rested and changed but if the same leg is always rested or a front leg is 'pointing' this could be a sign there is discomfort or injury.

- Not lame when walked and/or trotted up.

- If in a field, grazing happily with others.

- Normal behaviour for that individual horse.

The signs of ill-health are the opposite of the above.

Health and condition are not the same although they are related. Health is the well-being of a horse. Condition relates to a horse's state of fitness. If, however, a horse is in good condition for the work he is expected to do he will, of course, be in good health. A horse in good condition for competing a one-day event will look different from one who is doing a lot of slow work hacking around the countryside. The event horse will have more muscle and muscle tone and the horse who is only hacking gently will probably be carrying more weight.

Eating, drinking, breathing, the way in which a horse stands and the horse's droppings can all be indicators of a horse's state of health. A healthy horse will always

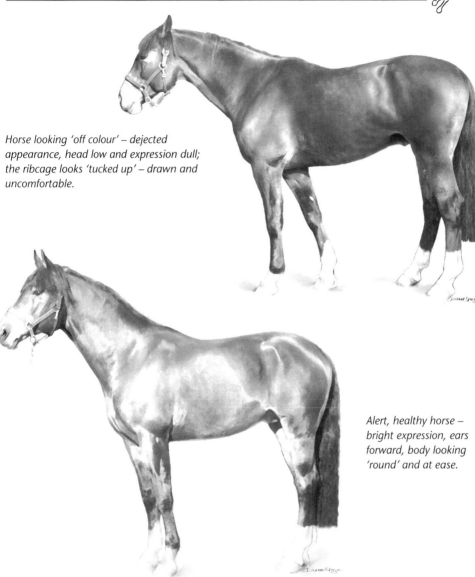

Horse looking 'off colour' – dejected appearance, head low and expression dull; the ribcage looks 'tucked up' – drawn and uncomfortable.

Alert, healthy horse – bright expression, ears forward, body looking 'round' and at ease.

be happy to eat. If a horse is off his food and the food is of good quality and his usual type then that is often a first sign that he is not feeling well. A horse standing in his box and breathing very quickly may be in pain, as long as he has not just worked or something has attracted his attention. If a horse is not passing droppings regularly he could be building up for a bout of colic. If he has very loose droppings there could have been a quick change of diet or access to rich pasture. As long as this does not carry on his system may well right itself, but if diarrhoea persists the vet should be called. If a horse is constantly moving around appearing uncomfortable, or looks as if he is trying to distribute his weight in a way that favours one leg, he is probably not feeling well and should be observed carefully for the next hour to see how things progress.

Checking for unsoundness

You will not be expected to assess a horse to see if he is unsound, but you need to be able to discuss the principles behind this. A horse should not be trotted up to identify the lame leg if he is lame in walk. When trotted up, if he is lame in a front leg, the horse will lift his head up when the lame leg comes to the ground. If you think of him saying 'Ouch' as the lame leg comes to the ground, his head comes up to indicate this.

Hind-leg lameness is more difficult to recognise. The horse's hip will lower more as the sound leg comes to the ground, as it will be taking more weight. As well as looking at the way in which the horse moves, you can also listen to the sound of his footfalls. They should be regular. Any irregularity will highlight a potential issue. Having the opportunity to trot the horse on hard and soft ground, uphill and downhill, can highlight different lameness issues.

Having found the lame leg, the first thing is to inspect the foot. Look for stones, foreign objects or injury. Then check for heat in the foot. Always compare the feet for heat. If one is hotter than the other then there is likely to be a problem in the foot with more heat. If there does not appear to be an issue in the foot then look and feel for heat, swelling or other injury up the legs. Again always compare each pair of legs. If you know all the lumps and bumps that a horse normally has then you will be able to recognise a new one more quickly.

Teeth

A horse has 12 incisors (front teeth for biting food) and 24 molars (back teeth for grinding). All male (and some female) horses have four tushes, and some horses also develop wolf teeth, which are close to the molar teeth.

The action of a horse grinding his molars leads to uneven wear of his teeth. The outsides of the top molar teeth and the insides of the bottom ones develop sharp projections. These can cause the horse pain by cutting into his cheeks. The uneven wear

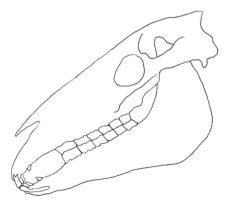

A horse has 12 incisor and 24 molar teeth.

can also lead to the horse 'quidding'. This is where the horse chews his food and, instead of swallowing it all, he drops large amounts out of his mouth. Consequently a horse should have his teeth checked every six months by a vet or a horse dentist and, if necessary, the molars rasped to remove the sharp edges.

Other signs of a horse having problems with his teeth might become evident when he is being ridden or tacked up. For example, he might show this by being unsteady in the head or mouth, by not wanting to open his mouth, by head-shaking, or by any other non-normal behaviour around his head/mouth region.

A young horse will lose his milk teeth (first set of teeth) between two and four years of age, when they are replaced by the permanent set. The eruption of the tushes and/or wolf teeth can lead to discomfort and the positioning of the bit must be watched carefully. Wolf teeth, which are usually very small, are often removed.

Minor wounds

There are five different types of minor wounds:

- **Bruise** Kicks, knocks or blows frequently cause bruises. The skin is often not broken. There may or may not be swelling and pain.

- **Graze** This is a 'skin scrape'. The top layer of skin is taken off, usually by friction. Often there is very little bleeding, but there could be numerous foreign objects in the wound.

- **Incision** This is a clean cut from something like a piece of glass or a knife.

Some types of wound.

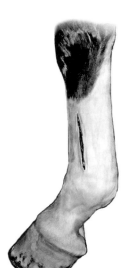

An incised wound   A laceration   A puncture wound

- **Laceration** This is a tear wound that will often have rough edges. Barbed wire or being caught on a hawthorn hedge can cause this type of wound.

- **Puncture** This wound has a very small entry point, but the wound can be deep. Often there can be a foreign body trapped inside and this can lead to infection.

The treatment for all minor wounds is similar:

1. Assess the wound. If it is a simple minor wound then the vet will probably not be necessary. (As long as the horse is vaccinated against tetanus.)

2. Stop the bleeding. This should be done by applying pressure to the wound. Something sterile is ideal, but if there is nothing sterile available then a clean piece of cloth is better than nothing.

3. Cleanse the wound. There are two ways to undertake this:

   (a) Trickle hosing. Using the hosepipe with a slow water pressure. To get the horse used to the hose, direct the water on the hoof first and slowly take it up the leg so that the water is flowing from just above the wound and running down over the wound. Hose for 10–20 minutes. This is a very effective way of cleaning a wound as well as helping to reduce inflammation.

(b) Using cotton wool and cooled, boiled, salt water. Use each piece of cotton wool only once so you do not cross-infect the wound. Be gentle but positive with the cotton wool and make sure you have removed all the foreign bodies from the wound before you start to dress it.

4. Dress the wound. If the wound is very small or is a bruise it may need no dressing at all. Leaving it open to the air will speed up the healing process. If the wound needs veterinary attention then do not put anything on it. The vet may want to stitch it and will be unable to do so if there is any form of ointment on it.

5. Check that the horse has up to date tetanus cover. If he does not, the vet must be called to administer the vaccination.

The principles of sick nursing

If a horse is ill or confined to his box through injury there are some basic rules you need to abide by to assist in a speedy recovery.

At all times the person looking after the horse must be observant and pay particular attention to detail.

- Ideally just one person should look after the horse – this leads to small changes in improvement or decline being noticed quickly.

- The vet's instructions must be followed exactly.

- The horse's environment must be clean. Bedding should be deep and clean. Short straw is best, as it will not get caught round the horse's legs. If there is a wound, shavings and similar beddings may stick to it and delay the healing process.

- The horse's box must be well-ventilated, but without draughts.

- The horse should be fed in small amounts and anything that is not eaten cleared away. Succulents often entice a sick horse to eat. The only time you should change a horse's diet suddenly is if he has to stop work because of an injury or illness. If he is confined to his box his hard feed must be cut straight away and the amount of bulk increased.

- The horse must have access to water. Change it frequently to ensure it is always clean and fresh.

- Keep the horse warm but not hot. Use lightweight rugs as necessary. Test how warm he is by feeling the base of his ears. Stable bandages may help to keep him comfortable and will encourage blood circulation.

- Do not fuss over the horse unnecessarily. When you are ill you probably like some attention, but you also want peace and quiet to rest!

- Keep clear records of the horse's condition, medication and progress.

- Do not groom as usual. A light brushing (if required) is sufficient. Keep the horse's eyes, nose and dock clean and his feet picked out.

- If permitted by the vet, or if appropriate, graze the horse in hand.

When to call the vet

When it comes to deciding when to call in the vet, a very experienced horse person may make a different decision from someone less experienced.

Generally you should call the vet when:

- There is any doubt as to what is wrong with a horse.

- There is a sharp rise in temperature with accompanying signs of illness or distress.

- There are signs of colic.

- There is a wound that needs stitching.

- There is a puncture wound.

- Arterial bleeding is present.

- The horse has a lameness that cannot be identified.

- The horse has a condition which, after a period of management, has not improved.

- Vaccinations are required.

- Medication is required.

You may be able to think of other times when you might call the vet. Make sure you have a good list of sensible suggestions so you can participate in the discussion.

Whenever you call the vet you should record this, and the treatment given, on the individual horse's record card. This is useful to see if there are any trends in the horse's health. This record card should also have the dates when the horse is due for vaccination, when he was last wormed (and with which type of wormer), when he was last shod and when his teeth were last rasped. The card should also record if he had any form of treatment, which was given by staff, even if the vet was not called. Without these records it is very difficult to ensure that everything is kept up to date.

Worming

Any horse can suffer from internal parasites, but it is possible to keep these to a minimum with good management. A horse with a heavy worm infestation may lose condition even if he eats well, may have a coat that does not have a shine, and may have a pot belly. He may be anaemic and have little energy. His droppings may be loose and smelly. Many cases of colic can be traced to a horse's worm burden. Such a horse will not be able to work to his true potential and food will be wasted. Horses can have a serious worm burden and not show these symptoms. Consequently it is important to have a worming programme for each horse.

Traditionally each horse was wormed every 6–8 weeks with different wormers to help prevent the larvae becoming resistant to the chemicals and to ensure all different types of parasites are treated. Current ideas have moved forward from this blanket approach to a more strategic methodology. Faecal egg counts are simple, easy and relatively cheap to undertake. Once you know the level of infestation and the types of larvae that are present you can then worm appropriately, if necessary with a targeted wormer. Undertaking worm counts approximately four times a year will give you information to ensure you are worming only if it is necessary and targeting the offending parasites.

The following are the most common internal parasites that infest horses:

- Large redworms

- Small redworms

- Roundworms

- Bots

- Threadworms

- Pinworms

- Lungworms

- Tapeworms

To ensure worm infestation is kept to a minimum it is important to ensure the horse's pasture is well managed. The daily picking up of droppings and not overgrazing the pasture are the best ways to keep infestation at bay.

What the assessor is looking for

- You must be able to look at a horse and describe the basic signs of good health. Try to be systematic in your description and then you won't forget anything. For example, start at the head and describe bright eyes, clear eyes and nose (no discharge) and mobile ears.

- Make quite sure that when you discuss condition with your assessor, he or she knows exactly what you are talking about because you explain it clearly.

- Be able to describe the horse's digestive system. Be very clear on the progression of food through the horse's gut. You may be required to pick up the discussion halfway through the process, so it is important that you listen to the other candidates and can carry on from wherever the person before you is asked to stop. A clear, basic understanding of the way each part of the system functions is important as it will help you to speak with confidence when describing the parts.

- Make sure that you know where in the horse's body each major organ lies. You should be able to indicate on the horse's body where a particular organ is and approximately how much room it takes up. The major organs that you are likely to be asked about include the heart, lungs, stomach, liver, kidneys and intestines. The stomach is approximately the size of a rugby ball.

- You may be asked about the importance of bulk to the function of the digestive system. Bulk enables the whole length of the digestive tract to keep moving. Without roughage there would be nothing to keep moving the other, softer or more easily rendered down materials through the system and it would slow down or stop.

- Know that the hind gut contains bacteria or 'gut flora' which assist in the digestion of the roughage in the diet. The health of the bacteria is partly dependent on the consistency of the horse's diet and the overall well-being of the horse.

- You must be familiar with the skeletal structure of the horse, and you are likely to be asked about this in a stable, with a horse in front of you. You must know not only the names of the bones but also where the bones are in the body as you look at the horse. Make sure that you have learned how many vertebrae there are, what the bones in the front and the hind legs are called, and learn them well. Guessing roughly where the bones are will not be good enough if you are asked to point them out exactly. Be able to pick up the discussion at any point – you may have to describe just the hind leg or a section of the back.

- Learn the horse's normal temperature, pulse and respiration rates and be able to relate these to his pattern of health.

- Know that an increase in the horse's normal breathing rate (at rest 8 to 12 breaths per minute) might indicate pain or distress, and, if linked to other symptoms, may indicate ill health.

- Be able to talk about how the horse's pattern of eating can reflect his good health or be a sign of change in his state of well-being. If a horse goes off his food for no apparent reason, with possible other developing symptoms, it may indicate a change in his state of good health.

- Know the appearance of 'normal' droppings and understand the changes in consistency and possible 'smell' that might indicate an impending change of health.

- Be able to recognise and discuss how a horse might stand if he is not healthy. Be aware that either constant moving around, apparently trying to find a comfortable stance, or an appearance that the horse is distributing weight awkwardly to 'save' one or more limbs, indicates a possible problem.

- Your knowledge of the skeleton must include the external parts of the foot. Be quite familiar and very practised at being able to describe each part of the foot and its basic function.

- Be aware of the existence of the 'white line'. Be sure that you can find it on the foot (easier to do on an unshod foot), and understand its importance in relation to where the farrier's nails are driven to hold a shoe in place.

- You must be able to describe the signs or symptoms of a horse that is unsound or lame.

- Basic wound treatment must be studied, and it is advisable to be able to describe the most up-to-date methods.

- You may be asked to discuss how you would care for a horse that is ill or perhaps confined to his box owing to injury. Good attention to detail would be essential to enable you to monitor the 'patient' closely. Good sick nursing would include having one person only to care for the horse and therefore be able to keep an ongoing check on the horse; fresh, deep bedding; fresh, clean water and feed; treatment according to the horse's condition, and veterinary advice if appropriate.

- You must have clear opinions about when you might need to call the vet as these could affect the well-being of a horse in your care.

- You should be able to discuss records that would essentially be maintained in any well-run yard. These would include some kind of system by which each horse in the yard had his own health records.

- You should be aware that horses suffer from parasitic worm infestations, and that some kind of worming programme is important. (A horse with a worm infestation may lose condition, have a stary coat and a 'pot' belly, and be not thriving generally.)

- Be sure that you can discuss several acceptable worming programmes for horses because today there is more than one opinion on effective worm management.

  You will be expected to show a knowledge of how often a horse's teeth should be checked and why. You must be aware that quidding is invariably a sign that something is wrong with the teeth and that it is imperative they are looked at by a professional. You are not expected to be able to age a horse by his teeth.

How to become competent

- This is a section where you must take the time and the trouble to learn the physiological terms for the various bones in the body and the parts and functions of the digestive system.

- Then spend time looking at a horse and indicating where on the body the respective parts of the skeleton and the various organs lie.

- This section of the syllabus is one area where you can work with another person who is studying for Stage 2, helping and testing each other.

- From time to time reinforce your learning with your coach/instructor, asking him/her to take you through the parts of the skeleton, the major organs and the digestive system, identifying correct locations and names.

- Practise picking up the skeleton or digestive system 'halfway through'. Be able to describe just the bones of the hind leg. Be able to carry on the discussion on the digestive system from the start of the small intestine or from the hind gut to the end.

- Look at the difficult names like 'oesophagus', 'duodenum' and 'ileum', familiarise yourself with their spelling and pronunciation; similarly with the 'cervical vertebrae', 'sesamoid bones' and 'scapula'. As soon as you struggle or seem uncomfortable over any of these terms, you indicate a lack of confidence and an unfamiliarity in using these words – and that shows your lack of preparation. If you find yourself next to someone who has prepared this area very thoroughly, you may feel inadequate and this will cause you to fumble and falter even more.

- If you are looking after one or more horses on a full-time basis, you will become very familiar with what is 'normal' for each horse in terms of health, well-being and behaviour. From this it is easy to recognise small signs of discomfort.

- Awareness of small changes and signs are the hallmark of a good horsemaster. Try to be observant of small indications, which might indicate the beginnings of a problem.

- Look at every horse that comes into the yard, whether at livery or to school, and consider his condition. Spend time watching horses moving (in the school under saddle, or when they are being led, even if this is only in or out of the field). You will then learn to recognise when a horse is irregular in his gaits.

- When you have the opportunity of handling or grooming any horse, get into the habit of running your hands down each of the four legs and feel how cool and un-puffy they are. If there are any slight lumps, bumps or swellings, ask your instructor to explain why they are there and whether they have a special name or not (e.g. windgalls). Get used to comparing the two front legs, and similarly the hind legs, to see whether any 'heat' you may feel in one leg is isolated or is the same in the opposite leg.

- Similarly with the feet, feel the wall of the hoof and compare both front feet and then both hind feet.

- Feeling heat and pain in a limb takes practice, as does improving your 'eye' for how the horse looks.

- Try to be involved in dealing with any minor wound treatments in the yard. In the event of a more serious incident, try to observe the management of the wound by senior members of staff and watch the vet work if he or she is called.

- Make sure that you have seen the yard records for each horse. Discuss with your instructor or the yard manager how the records are maintained and ask what sort of information is recorded and why.

- Make sure that you know what worming programme is used in your yard. Watch the worm doses being given and look at the products being used; ask your instructor why a certain product is used at that time of the year.

- Consider also what other measures are in place in your establishment to manage the pasture, which in turn assists in the control of worms.

- Find out how often the horses in your yard have their teeth checked and who treats them.

- When it comes to studying horse health, try to gain hands-on experience as well, as this will make it more 'real' and applicable. Ask questions about every aspect of horse health relevant to the above requirements and make sure that you look at as many horses as possible, especially if you have the chance to see some horses whose worm management may have been neglected.

UNIT 2b

The Principles of Shoeing, Clipping and Trimming Horses

4 Credits

Clipping, Trimming and Shoeing

The candidate should know:

The reasons for clipping and relevant welfare issues

How to assemble and maintain clippers

Why and how to pull manes and tails

Why and how to trim horses

The procedure for shoeing, including the use of farrier's tools

The procedure for removing a twisted shoe in an emergency

Clipping

Reasons for and frequency of clipping

- To remove some or all of the winter coat so the horse can work with less stress and not sweat so much.

- To help the horse to dry off more quickly after work and so prevent chills and colds.

- To make grooming easier.

- For appearance – the horse looks smarter with a clip.

- Sometimes it is necessary to clip a region of the horse to help treat skin or medical conditions.

- Traditionally the first clip is done in late September/early October, and the horse will be clipped as often as is necessary throughout the winter months until January. This may be once every three weeks, but could be more or less depending on how cold it is and how quickly the horse's coat grows. It is better not to clip the horse after the end of January as there is the possibility of the summer coat being spoiled. There are, however, times when a horse will need to be clipped later in the year. A horse working hard, e.g. a hunter or top-level eventer, may need this so he does not lose too much condition.

- Rugs must be used to replace the horse's coat that has been clipped off. Monitoring of the base of the ears will tell you if the horse is warm enough; if he is the coat will grow back more slowly and you will not have to clip him so often.

- Horses and ponies that live out all winter should not be clipped. Horses should not be clipped unnecessarily.

> NOTE: Potentially there is an element of danger in clipping a horse, especially one you do not know or one that has not been clipped before. This danger can be minimised by following safety rules and careful preparation.

The clipping area

A large, well-lit loosebox is required, with a non-slip floor. Rubber matting is ideal. If this is not available then a small amount of bedding should be left on the floor. The water bucket should be taken out. Some people tie up a haynet to keep the horse occupied; others feel that the horse moves too much when pulling at a net. The choice is personal so do whatever suits you and your horse. A rug should be available so that the horse does not have to stand and get cold immediately after being clipped while one is found. There needs to be a source of power nearby if you are using electric clippers. Some yards will tie a piece of string from the ceiling so that the cable can be threaded through it and come from above. There is then less possibility of the cable being trodden on. There must be a circuit-breaker between the plug and the electric socket. It may be necessary to have a strong box to stand on if the horse is being clipped towards the top of his head.

The horse

The horse must be clean and dry. Some people put on a tail bandage to ensure the dock area of the tail is not accidentally caught by the clippers. The mane can be plaited in 'dreadlocks' for the same reason. The desired clip can be 'drawn' on the horse with tailor's chalk or saddle soap. A very experienced person will be able to clip 'by eye'.

The handlers

Rubber-soled boots/shoes are a useful precaution from electric shock. Overalls are a sensible form of clothing as the clipped hair tends to get everywhere. A headscarf/cap may be worn for the same reason. If you have a horse you do not know, or a difficult horse, the wearing of a hard hat is recommended.

It is always advisable to have an assistant when clipping. The assistant should wear similar clothes but also needs gloves available just in case the horse starts to get fractious and he/she needs to hold the rope firmly. It would also be sensible for the assistant to wear a hard hat. The assistant should always stand on the same side of the horse as the person who is clipping and needs to be a competent horse handler.

The clippers

Always check that the clippers are working before you start clipping. Have machine oil available, a soft brush, a piece of cloth and a set of spare blades. A bowl of surgical spirit or blade wash should also be to hand. Make sure both sets of blades are sharp. Read the manufacturer's instructions. Put a set of blades onto the clippers and adjust to the correct tension. Do this in a safe place, taking care not to drop the blades and risk losing the spring. Different makes of blades have different tension settings. Always follow the operating instructions to set the tension. Make sure the machine is plugged into a circuit-breaker. Switch on the machine and oil the blades and put oil in the oil holes. Then switch the machine off. Wipe the excess oil from the blades and you should be ready to start.

> NOTE: It is really important that you know how to put clipper blades together – which way up they go, where the spring fits and the correct fitting of the screw. It is not unknown for some candidates to come to an examination never having handled a pair of clippers. This weakness will always be exposed on the day.

How to clip

When you have everything prepared as above it is important to try to make the whole experience as stress-free as possible for the horse. With the assistant holding the horse, switch on the clippers and allow a little time for him to get used to the noise. Do not start clipping straight away. Switch off the clippers and run them down the horse's neck so he can feel the metal against his skin. Switch the clippers back on and, if he does not worry about the noise, then hold the clippers against his skin so he can feel the vibration. Time taken to accustom the horse to the clippers will be timed saved in the long run. Do not start to clip before the horse accepts all the above.

Start the actual clip on the shoulder and neck, running the clippers against the lie of the hair. Make the strokes as long and as smooth as possible. You need to feel the horse's skin on the back of the clipper blades, but you should have the feeling of gliding over the skin rather than pushing deeply into it.

Whilst clipping, frequently test the clipper blades on the back of your hand to check that they are not getting too hot. Hot clipper blades will make the horse fidgety. If the blades get too hot then stop for a while and let them cool down. The clipper blades should be kept free from clipped hair, as should the air vents of the machine. The oil holes should be oiled regularly throughout the clipping process. The blades need to be brushed off and put through the blade wash occasionally to keep them clean and functional. The more efficient you are at clipping, the quicker the task will be done and the easier it is for all concerned. Every time you stop to assess how your clipping is going get into the habit of turning off the clippers to help keep them cool.

Once the neck and shoulders are clipped, the belly and back can be done as per the required clip. Do this both sides. To clip around the elbow and chest the assistant needs to hold up the front leg, pull it forward and hold it stretched out. It is then much easier to clip as the skin is pulled taut.

If you decide it is necessary to clip the horse's face it may be advisable to use small battery-operated clippers.

When clipping the area at the top of the tail it is usual to leave an inverted triangle shape. This ensures everything looks tidy and the tail is not caught by the clippers.

If you have a difficult horse to clip it may be advisable to take off only a minimum amount of hair. If this is not practical then offering him a feed may help. Holding up a front leg can help to keep him still. Asking an experienced person to twitch his nose can be very effective, but this must not be undertaken by a novice. The last resort is sedating the horse, although this can create problems in that it may make him sweat and the vet may not be available at the time you require him. It is better to try patience and calm

Type of clip.

Hunter clip – traditionally used for a horse that is hunting

Trace clip – this can be used for ponies and horses spending some time out in a field as well as doing moderate work

Chaser clip – this can be used for a horse in work that is likely to spend time standing around e.g. in a riding school

Blanket clip – this is useful for horses working quite hard but also spending some time turned out

Neck and belly clip – this is ideal for woolly ponies that do occasional work to stop them from sweating too much

Full clip – this clip is usually only used for horses in consistent, very hard work: sometimes hunters are fully clipped for their first clip and then a hunter clip is used after that

handling over a period of time. This invariably works, but may take a long time, especially if the horse has had a bad experience when being clipped. It is always better to start a horse off gently and slowly the first few times he is clipped, then the difficulties do not usually arise.

When you have finished clipping the horse he can be wiped over with a stable rubber, rugged up and put back into his own box. The clipping box should be tidied up, the clippers dismantled, cleaned and the blades sent away for re-sharpening if necessary. Clipping machines should be serviced annually.

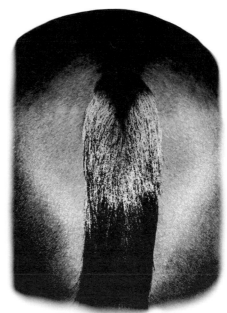

An inverted 'V' of unclipped hair ensuring the top of the tail is not damaged when clipping.

Pulling the mane

Mane pulling is undertaken principally for aesthetic reasons. Once a mane is pulled it is easier to plait and groom, and it looks tidier because it is thinner and shorter and so can lie flat on the horse's neck. Horses and ponies who live out all year round should not have their manes pulled as it helps to keep the neck and head warmer. Native ponies who are going to be shown should not have their manes pulled.

A mane should be pulled as often as is necessary. It is best done after exercise as the pores of the horse's skin will be more open and the hair should come out more easily. If a horse is having his mane pulled for the first time it may not be possible to do it all in one go – be patient and undertake the task over a period of days or even weeks. It is much better to have the horse on your side to undertake the task. Some horses are extremely sensitive and dislike having their manes pulled; others do not mind at all.

Pulling a mane using a comb.

Procedure for pulling a mane

- Tie the horse up. If you know he does not like the task it may be better to have an assistant to help you. You need a metal mane comb (with short teeth), a body brush and, if the horse is big, something secure to stand on. As with plaiting, the task is much easier if you are at the correct height. Brush the whole mane through with the body brush to take out any tangles.

- It does not matter whether you start at the poll or the withers. If you know the horse does not like one area it is better to start there and get that bit done. As you pull and approach the sensitive area (poll or withers) the horse will become more and more unsettled, so if that area is done first it is out of the way and finished. If the horse is not bothered then it might be an idea to start at the poll and work downwards. It will be easier on your arms to start with the most tiring part, i.e. the highest.

- Take hold of a small amount of long hair on the underside of the mane and backcomb the hair above it up towards the crest. Then pull out those long hairs on the underside of the mane you are holding. Some people pull these hairs out with their fingers; others twist them round the comb and use this to pull with. This method does help to protect your fingers.

- Do not pull hairs from the topside of the mane. They will grow back straight and spiky! Do not forget to pull the forelock in the same manner.

- Once the mane is fully pulled to the thinness and length you require it is easier to keep on top of it by pulling a few hairs at a time on a daily basis.

The lie of the mane

Tradition says that the mane should be on the offside of the horse. Plaiting in 'dreadlocks' will help to set a mane this way. A neck cover can also help to keep a mane flat and tidy. Some horses' manes will not stay to the offside no matter what you do. This really does not matter as long as you are not going to show your horse.

Thinning combs

There are a variety of thinning combs on the market that have some form of blade in them. These do not actually thin the mane; they tend just to make it shorter. They are very useful for horses that hate having their mane pulled. They can tidy up the mane, but if it is going to be plaited you may still have a very thick mane with plaits that may end up looking like golf balls when finished!

Pulling the tail

Tail pulling is undertaken to improve the appearance of the horse. In showing it is used to ensure the judge has a good view of the horse's hindquarters. As with mane pulling, horses that live out all year round should not have their tail pulled nor should native ponies that are being shown. A full tail gives protection from wind and inclement weather. If a tail is to be plaited then it should not be pulled.

Procedure for pulling a tail

- When pulling a tail make sure the horse is restrained as necessary. Always stand to the side of the horse's hindquarters and make sure you are not trapped in a corner of the stable.

- Brush the tail out thoroughly. Starting at the top of the tail, take a few hairs from the side of the tail, wrap them round the mane comb and pull them out. If the tail has not been pulled before it is probably better, as with the mane, to complete the task over a few days. Do not pull too much from the front of the tail or it can start to look

A neatly shaped tail.

89

bald! Some people use a razor to shave off tail hairs, but this should not be done as it can completely spoil the look, and the point where the shaving stops is very noticeable.

- Once a tail has been pulled it can be dampened and a tail bandage applied for a while to help set the required shape.

Trimming

Trimming is undertaken again to give the horse a smarter appearance. Generally it is undertaken with blunt-ended scissors and a mane comb. The areas you might trim would be :

- The hairs that stick out from the ears. Do not trim in the ears themselves as this hair helps to protect against infection. Put on the horse's headcollar and, if possible, get an assistant to hold him. Hold the sides of his ears together so the ear closes up. Then trim along this line, cutting off the hairs that protrude.

- Heels can be trimmed to remove the long hairs that grow down around the ergot. Take a mane comb and your blunt-ended scissors. Use the comb to brush the long hairs away from the fetlock and then trim upwards with the scissors.

- The hair that grows down around the coronary band can be trimmed with the blunt-ended scissors. A neat line round the top of the coronary band should be made. It is important not to damage the coronary band when undertaking this, and horses and ponies that live out should not be trimmed in this way.

- The long hairs that grow along the line of the bottom of the mandible can be trimmed with blunt-ended scissors or clipped with clippers to follow the line of the bottom jaw. A comb and scissors will give a more natural look.

- Some people cut off the whiskers around the nose and mouth, but this is not advisable as they are sensory organs that help a horse to feel for his food. Similarly

Trimming the long hairs of a horse's ears.

with the 'whiskers' around the eye. These are designed to help the horse from getting too close to something that will injure his eye.

- Thick feathers can be removed with clippers, moving against the lie of the hair. This is a labour-saving method and, for some horses with very thick feathers, the task would be beyond a pair of scissors. Again, though, for a more natural look, scissors are better. This should not be done with native ponies that are going to be shown or those living out all year.

The shoeing procedure

- The farrier usually removes a front shoe first. The relevant horse's foot is held between the farrier's legs, leaving both hands free. The farrier puts the buffer under a clench and, with the driving hammer, knocks the clench end up. This is done for all the clenches so the ends are all straight and no longer bent over onto the wall of the hoof.

- The farrier then takes the pincers and levers off the shoe, starting with the outside heel and moving the pincers forward away from the hoof. The farrier then moves to the other heel and does the same thing, then moves to the quarter of the outside of the shoe and prises that forward, then the quarter on the inside. Finally the farrier places the pincers at the toe of the shoe and prises the whole shoe off.

- The farrier then takes the hoof cutters and cuts off the excess foot growth.

- The drawing knife is then used to tidy up the foot and the frog.

- The rasp is then used to level off the foot.

- The drawing knife is then used to make a gap in the hoof wall for the toe clip (in a front foot). (For a back foot it will usually be two quarter clips.)

- While the farrier is doing this the shoe will be heating up in the forge (unless, of course, the horse is being cold shod, in which case this will not be done). Hot shoeing tends to ensure a closer/tighter and generally a better fit for the shoe, so is usually preferred.

- When the shoe is red-hot the farrier will use a pair of tongs to take the shoe to the anvil.

The farrier's tools.

Drawing/paring knife – trims the horn, sole and frog

Driving hammer – used with buffer to raise clenches; hammers nails into hoof; trims the ends of nails

Clenching tongs or nail clencher – folds the nail ends over so the clench is flush with the hoof wall

Rasp – levels the surface of the foot and finishes off around the edge once the shoe is on

Pritchel – carries the hot shoe from the anvil to the foot

Buffer – raises clenches

Pincers – levers off the shoe

Hoof cutters – trim the hoof (one side has a sharp blade; the other has a square end acting as a block)

- The shoe is hammered on the anvil to approximately the correct shape and size and then a pritchel is driven into one of the nail holes. This is used to carry the shoe to the foot.

- The shoe is then burned onto the foot. The marks created show the farrier how well the shoe fits and how flat the foot is.

- If necessary the shoe is re-shaped on the anvil and checked again on the foot.

- Once the farrier is happy with one shoe the process will be repeated with the other three.

- All four shoes will then be immersed in water to cool them.

- The shoes are then secured onto the foot. Traditionally there are four nails on the outside

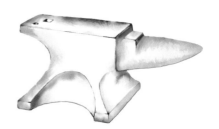

Anvil – an iron block upon which the shoes are shaped.

of a shoe and three on the inside. A farrier will, however, put in as many nails as is necessary. It is usually desirable to put fewer nails on the inside of the foot so there is less possibility of the horse damaging himself if the clenches start to rise. The first nail to be put in will be one at the toe. This helps to ensure the shoe does not slip. If the farrier first puts in a nail at the heel there is a much stronger possibility of the shoe slipping.

- Once each nail is hammered in (between the outside of the hoof and the white line) the farrier will twist off the end so that there is only a short length of nail left to work with.

- Once all the nails are hammered in, the farrier will take the rasp and smooth off the twisted edges of the nails and will also make a 'bed' for each nail in the hoof wall.

- The clenching tongs will then be used to make the clenches from the nail ends. Some farriers use the pincers under the nail head and the driving hammer on the nail end to create each clench.

- The toe clip is then knocked into place with the hammer.

- The rasp is then used around the junction of the hoof and shoe and the hoof wall to ensure there are no gaps and the whole foot is neat and tidy. The less pronounced side of the rasp is used for this task so the hoof wall is not damaged.

- The process is repeated for all four feet.

- It is useful to trot the horse up after shoeing to check that the horse does not have a nail bind. (This is where the nail is close to the white line and putting pressure on it. The farrier will usually know if a nail has pricked the horse in the sensitive part of the foot because there will be a reaction from the horse and often blood on the nail.)

Showing how to remove a twisted shoe

For Stage 2 you need to know how to remove a shoe in an emergency and may be asked to act out the procedure during your exam.

- Take the driving hammer, buffer and pincers. Make sure the horse is tied up, or

*The different methods of securing the front and hind foot so that hands
are free to remove a shoe.*

bringing hoof
between legs
(front foot)

securing leg
over one thigh
(hind foot)

somebody is holding him. Ask another candidate to hold the pincers while you have the hammer and buffer. If it is a front shoe, stand and face backwards (with your back to the horse's shoulders) and put the leg between your thighs so that you have it secure. You can then demonstrate how to use the buffer and hammer to lift all the clenches. Do not actually try to do this, just go through the motions near to each clench. The assessor will be looking at how you hold the horse's leg and how confident you are with the tools. Then exchange the hammer and buffer for the pincers. Again, just going through the motions, hold the pincers at the outside heel, bend them forwards, then repeat at the inside heel, then at the quarters, then at the toe. If it is a hind leg, remember (once you have collected your tools) first to go to the horse's head and stroke him on the neck before you move to pick up the hind leg. To do this, bend your knees a little and rest the fetlock on the thigh that is nearer to the horse. Do not put a hind leg through your thighs in case the horse tries to kick.

The consequences of leaving shoes on too long

Some of the problems that can be experienced when a shoe is left on too long are:

- The foot will overgrow the shoe, which can lead to friction, bruising and slipping when the foot touches the ground.

- The foot will grow too long altering, the hoof/pastern angle, which can lead to joint, tendon, ligament and hoof issues, i.e. the foot balance will no longer be correct.

- The wall of the hoof can become damaged.

- The sole may end up closer to the ground, thus making bruising more likely.

- The horse is more likely to lose a shoe when working.

A long toe.

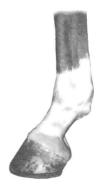

A recently shod foot.

Importance of regular trimming for unshod horses

Horses and ponies that are unshod, either because they are not working or they are working on surfaces from which their feet do not need protection, should still have their feet trimmed regularly. The natural wear through working is insufficient to maintain soundness. Trimming helps to maintain the shape of the foot, hence the foot balance is retained and a level bearing surface sustained. Many ponies have hard feet and work perfectly well without shoes. Their feet must be checked daily for stones and debris and observed to make sure they are not starting to go 'footsore'. Many riding schools put front shoes only on their horses. This helps to cut down on injuries from kicking in the fields, keeps farriery costs lower and works very well if the horses work on soft going such as an artificial surface or bridleways most of the time.

What the assessor is looking for

- You should know the reasons for clipping and how often you would need to clip a horse to keep him looking really tidy. The assessor will be looking for evidence of practical experience in handling horses and clippers. This will come through in the confidence you show when handling the equipment and the care you take with the clippers and all the associated parts. For instance, if the clippers have a handle, make sure you put your hand through it so that if you should lose your grip you will not drop them on the floor.

- You should be familiar with the range of clips that are given to horses, according to the work they are doing and the conditions under which they are kept. You may be asked to identify a particular clip on a horse that is brought out in front of you, or to indicate on a horse where the hair would be removed and where it would remain. If asked to describe a blanket clip, for example, then you would suggest that this is ideal for a horse that is working quite hard but may also have to stand around at a competition and therefore needs some warmth over his back.

- You may be asked about safety when clipping, including what clothing might be appropriate and where would be a safe area in which to clip. You should be able to demonstrate your position in the stable with relation to the horse while clipping him. You may be asked about what assistance you might need when clipping the horse's head or under his belly, and what practical means of restraining him would be appropriate if he objected to being clipped.

- Show an ability to pull a mane and a tail correctly. This would include showing an understanding that horses vary in their sensitivity to having their manes and tails pulled.

- Knowledge of when it is appropriate to pull manes and tails, and trim areas such as heels and ears, would be expected. You probably will not actually have to pull or trim a horse. You may have to partially undertake the process, and you will certainly have to discuss it. In your discussion you should speak from actual experience and talk about the issues you have come across.

- You should be able to describe the order and procedure in which the farrier removes the shoes, dresses the horse's foot, and prepares and replaces the new or refitted shoes.

- Know thoroughly the tools that the farrier uses, the order in which they are used and the specific use of each tool.

- Feel confident that you can demonstrate how you would pick up a front and a hind foot, and can handle the necessary tools to remove a shoe in an emergency.

- Be able to describe the problems that the horse is likely to experience if the shoes are left on for too long.

How to become competent

- You may not have the opportunity to actually clip a horse but you must assist someone and ask them to allow you to use the clippers on a large part of the horse (flank or neck) so that you have actually handled the machinery.

- If you are in a full-time training situation, particularly in a commercial yard, you will almost certainly have the opportunity to practise the skills of clipping and trimming, which must be demonstrated to you in a 'hands-on' situation.

- Take the time to watch someone pulling a mane and tail. There is a skill and technique involved, which comes from watching someone competent and then practising yourself.

- If you have a chance to go into a yard where horses are prepared for showing classes then you will see manes and tails pulled and heels trimmed to a very high standard.

- Competence in clipping comes with practice. Make sure that you have handled the clipping machine as much as possible. Each brand of clippers is slightly different, but they are all largely similar. Read the manufacturer's instructions to ensure you have the correct tension for the blades. Practise removing the blades and replacing them. Take particular care not to lose any of the tiny parts. Always handle the blades either close to the floor (in a squatting position) or over a table, so that if you do drop any of the pieces they do not bounce off into oblivion and you lose them. Cutting blades can shatter easily if dropped.

- When you first start clipping, draw an outline of the clip on the horse using chalk or saddle soap. This allows you to follow the line easily, rather than having to clip it 'freehand' (which is unwise if you are not experienced). Use a numnah to outline the saddle patch if you are clipping the horse for a hunter clip.

- Start the clipping procedure on an 'easy' part of the horse – the shoulder or the neck – before progressing to areas where he might be more fractious. In the early stages of learning to clip ask someone more competent than you to assist and give you moral support.

- Make sure you know why a particular type of clip is used. If in doubt, ask questions. Frequency of clipping depends on many factors, including the time of year, amount of coat growth, weather, conditions in which the horse is kept (in or out), and how tidy you need him to look.

- Make sure you feel competent about assisting with clipping, especially in such roles as pulling a horse's front leg forward and taut so the tricky area around the elbow can be clipped.

- It is absolutely essential that you watch a farrier working as often as you can.

- The more familiar you are with the adept way in which your farrier removes a horse's shoes, the better.

- Familiarise yourself completely with all the tools the farrier uses, know their names and the order in which they are used.

- You can read up on this subject but also ask questions of your farrier to gain your genuine practical knowledge.

- Make sure that you have handled the tools required to remove a shoe (buffer, driving hammer and pincers).

- Make sure that you regularly practise picking up and holding a front foot and, in turn, a hind foot in such a way that you can use the tools effectively to remove a shoe.

- When your farrier is not too busy and in a hurry to get to the next client, ask if you can practise removing a shoe.

- With both a hind and fore foot you need to be able to support the leg and foot in such a way that your hands are free to use the tools to remove the shoe.

- If you watch the farrier you will see exactly how this is done, then you must practise. Make sure you are not wearing your best breeches when doing this as you will ruin them. When you demonstrate this procedure in your exam, pick up a stable rubber (or cloth) and cover your knee to protect your clean breeches. (Farriers wear a leather apron!)

- In your day-to-day handling of the horse (you should be routinely caring for the feet at least twice a day, picking them out) be observant of the ongoing condition of the feet. If looking at the feet of a new horse, make sure that you take careful note of their condition and the state of the shoes.

UNIT 3a

The Principles of Watering, Feeding and Fittening Horses

6 Credits

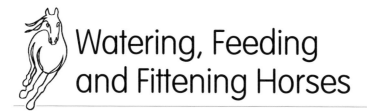

Watering, Feeding and Fittening Horses

The candidate should know:

The rules of watering and understand their reasons

The rules of feeding and understand their reasons

A variety of feedstuffs, their preparation and suitability for horses

About feeding bulk food

How to produce a feed chart

How to get a turned away horse fit for non-stressful exercise up to one-and-a-half hours a day

How to care for a horse after work

How to 'rough off' a horse

This section is assessed in the theory part of the exam. Although all parts of the theory are important, watering and feeding are seen as vital and must be discussed accurately, with genuine practical knowledge shown.

Watering

Rules of watering

The rules of watering are as follows:

- A clean, constant supply of fresh water should always be available, unless a vet advises otherwise in the case of ill-health.

- Water should be changed regularly to avoid a build-up of ammonia.

- All water containers should be scrubbed regularly and kept clean. Again this helps to avoid a build-up of ammonia and encourages the horse to drink.

A strong bucket well placed in a corner of the stable.

- Water before feeding – this is a rather old-fashioned rule. It comes from the days when horses did not have free access to water and were taken to a trough regularly to drink. If they were taken for a drink after they had eaten they would drink a lot and the food would be washed through the system quickly without all the nutrients being taken into the body. There could also be the possibility of the food swelling and causing colic. Nowadays horses have free access to water so they tend not to want to take a long draught after eating.

- A horse should not be allowed a long drink when he is very hot, or straight after hard work. This can lead to colic. Giving him small amounts every 15 minutes is far more beneficial as is giving water with the chill taken off. Once he no longer appears thirsty he can be given free access to water again.

- Horses should not be allowed to drink from sandy-bottomed streams. Sand may be ingested leading to sand colic.

- Water troughs in fields must be checked daily to ensure a constant supply of water.

*An unsafe bucket. The handle is left towards the horse and he could
catch himself on it.*

- All water containers must be safe. Buckets should have their handles turned towards the wall and troughs should have no sharp edges.

- If going to a competition it is advisable to take your own water so the horse is not put off drinking by water tasting and smelling different from that which he is used to.

- Monitor the horse's intake of water. Between 60% and 70% of the horse's body is water, which is constantly being lost and so must be replaced. With buckets it is easy to monitor what the horse is drinking, but in the field with a communal trough and in stables with automatic waterers it is more difficult. Some yards, however, do have meters attached to individual automatic waterers.

Watering systems

In a loosebox there are two main ways of providing water for a horse.

- Buckets should be made of rubber or heavy plastic. They should be placed in a corner of the box. Some people put them in a tyre to help stop the horse knocking them over, but this can take up a lot of room in the stable. If buckets are used it is easy to monitor the amount of water the horse drinks. They are also easy to scrub clean daily. If medicine has to be administered in water it is easy to do this and to ensure it has been drunk. Water bucket handles can be a hazard and they should always be placed towards the wall.

Buckets are labour-intensive. They can be time-consuming to fill and heavy to lift and carry. Some people have buckets that clip to the wall. These put the horse's head in an unnatural position to drink and also can create more of a hazard in the box.

- Automatic waterers are labour-saving and ensure the horse is never without water. They must, however, be regularly maintained and the pipes should be lagged to try to stop them freezing in the winter. They can be difficult to clean and, as mentioned earlier, without expensive meters being attached it is not possible to monitor how much a horse is drinking. They must be carefully positioned in a loosebox or they can create a hazard. Some automatic bowls are quite small and do not allow the horse to take a long drink if he wants one.

In a field there are several ways that water can be provided for horses.

- The best way is with a carefully sited self-filling trough. The trough should not be placed under a tree – it will become contaminated with leaves. It should not be placed near the field entrance, as this is an area that is already prone to poaching – placing the trough near the gate will lead to more poaching. Any form of trough needs to be scrubbed out regularly. Automatic troughs need to be regularly maintained – if there is a malfunction with the mechanism the trough can overflow, lose a lot of water and create a muddy patch. In freezing conditions they can freeze over and the ice needs to be broken several times a day.

- A river may seem the ideal way to provide water for a horse, but there are many problems with this. The water may have been contaminated upstream and there is no way of knowing this without regular, expensive water-testing. The river may be prone to flooding. The access may not be safe and will probably become poached. If the river has a sandy bottom the horse can ingest sand and this may cause colic.

- A pond is likely to be stagnant and the water therefore unfit for consumption. Horses should not be allowed access and so ponds should be securely fenced off.

- Buckets are usually used in a field only as a last resort. There is a lot of hard work involved in refilling and carrying buckets for a field. Invariably they will be knocked over and the water wasted, leaving the horses without.

- Troughs that do not refill automatically must be regularly cleaned and refilled. The easiest way to do this is with a hosepipe. Troughs should be safe with no sharp edges on which horses can injure themselves.

Feeding

Rules of feeding and their importance

Over the last few years a great deal of research has been undertaken into feeding horses, but there are a number of basic principles that have not altered. A horse receives energy from food and this is required for maintenance of life, growth and/or work and repair of tissue. The horse has a complicated digestive system. If the basic rules of feeding are applied they will help maintain the functioning of the system and hence a healthy, happy horse.

- **Feed according to work undertaken, age, type, body weight, temperament, time of year, level of rider.** This is probably the most important rule. If you overfeed a horse he can become too fresh. It can also lead to digestive disorders and filled legs. The horse can also become obese. If you do not feed a horse enough he will not thrive and will be unable to do the work you require of him.

- **Feed little and often.** A horse has a small stomach relative to his size (about the size of a rugby ball). In the wild he is a trickle feeder and feeding him little and often mimics this.

- **Feed plenty of bulk.** This will ensure that the digestive system will continue to work. It also again helps to mimic the horse's natural eating habits and stops him becoming bored when in the stable.

- **Always feed good quality forage.** Feeding poor quality, cheap food is a false economy. The horse may well not eat it. If he does it may lead to colic or respiratory disorders.

- **Keep to a regular routine.** The horse is a creature of habit and thrives on routine. This also helps to aid digestion.

- **Make changes to food gradually.** The horse has many different types of bacteria in his gut, which break down the food ingested. These bacteria are 'food-type specific' and the more of one type of feed you give the horse, the more of that bacteria type there will be. If you suddenly change the type of feed, the existing gut bacteria may not be able to cope with it, and this can lead to problems such as colic. If you change food type gradually the bacteria have the opportunity to multiply to sufficient numbers to deal with the food.

- **Keep all utensils and equipment clean.** You would not want to eat your meals off a dirty plate or have your meals prepared with unclean utensils. Keeping everything clean ensures food is not contaminated.

- **Feed something succulent every day.** Horses enjoy apples and carrots and find them appetising; they also help to provide vitamins and minerals.

- **Feed at least one hour before exercise.** If the horse has a full stomach it will press on the diaphragm, impair breathing and lead to the horse not being able to perform to the best of his abilities. Think how you would feel trying to undertake an active task with a full stomach.

- **Do not feed straight after exercise.** During exercise, blood is pushed to the muscles and away from the digestive organs. Once the horse has cooled down his metabolism and blood supply will have returned to normal.

Assessing feed samples

Whole oats.

Whole barley.

When assessing the quality of feed the sample should be a good colour, bright and clean. It should not be dusty. It should be dry and give a pleasant, sweet smell. Some feed samples have been in jars for a long time and, when you take the lid off to examine them, it is not a good idea to put your nose in the jar and take a deep breath. The sample may be very dusty.

If you are given a sample of hay to assess, there should be good quality grasses in it with no weeds or poisonous plants.

You need to know some feedstuffs that are heating and some that are fattening. Some examples of feeds that have a heating effect are:

- maize

- oats

- peas

- beans

- some compound feeds such as event/racehorse cubes/mixes

Some examples of feeds that have a fattening effect are:

- barley

- linseed

- some compound feeds and conditioning cubes

Feedstuffs suitable for horses doing fast work are such feeds as oats, peas and beans, alfalfa, lucerne and compound mixes designed especially for this kind of work. It must be remembered, however, that some horses may well be able to undertake fast work on 'non-heating' food. Consequently it may be said that most feeds are suitable if the horse is provided with sufficient energy for the work he is required to do and he is not over- or under-weight. It is generally accepted, though, that some more fattening feeds are best avoided in large quantities, e.g. sugar beet. Sugar beet can, however, be very useful as part of a horse's feeding regime and should not be automatically excluded because of its reputation!

Feeding a horse/pony living at grass

The majority of the horse's diet will be bulk. In winter the grass will have little or no nutritional value and may well be in very short supply. Hay and haylage are the best supplementary food, although some people feed oat straw to ponies, if available. This extra food is best fed twice daily and in piles far enough apart so the horses cannot reach each other to fight. Make sure you put out one more pile than there are horses, so that if there is one individual that is likely to be bullied there is always a pile for him to go to.

It may also be necessary to feed hard feed depending on the amount of work the horses are doing and the type of animals they are. Some horses may not need any, but others may need up to 25% of their feed ration as hard feed to keep them in good condition. Compound feeds like horse and pony nuts are probably the easiest to feed, although straight feeds like barley (bruised, micronised or rolled) and sugar beet can be useful.

In spring the grass will start to grow. The horses will let you know when they no longer need hay, as they will leave it in preference to the grass. It is very important, especially if the grass is lush, that grazing is restricted for good doers. Ponies are especially prone to laminitis and it is better to restrict their access to grass rather than have to deal with a laminitic animal. Horses kept on quality grazing during the spring may well not need any concentrate food.

In summer again, as long as the grazing is well maintained, there may not be any necessity to feed concentrate food. If the summer is very dry, the grass will not grow and the animals may need hay and hard feed to ensure they maintain condition and their ability to work. Flies and other insects can be a real nuisance and horses need some form of shelter from them. If stables are available some people turn out during the night and bring the horses in during the day to keep them out of the heat and protected from insects.

In early autumn there can be a flush of grass and a careful eye must be kept on those animals prone to laminitis. After this, the quality and amount of grass will start to decline and it is necessary to monitor the condition of the horses, feeding hay/haylage and hard feed as required to ensure they do not lose condition.

Feeding old and sick horses

In the exam this takes the form of a general discussion of basic principles and, as with all feeding of horses, every animal is an individual and what suits one horse may not be acceptable to another.

Old horses tend not to utilise the food they are given as efficiently as younger horses. They may become fussy feeders. This can mean they become 'poor doers'. They may have problems with biting and chewing food. Feeding them foods that are soft and palatable will encourage them to eat more. They may prefer meadow hay as it is softer and sweeter than seed hay. They may not want to eat large amounts of food, so they may need feeding more frequently. Consequently they need good quality and very nutritious food. Boiled barley with linseed, sugar beet and compound feeds are useful. Some manufacturers produce feeds especially for older horses.

Sick horses may not want to eat. There also may be medicine to be administered via the food. Consequently it is important that the food offered is highly palatable and easy to digest. It is much better to offer a sick horse very small feeds at frequent intervals. Any food not eaten should be removed. Hand feeding grated apples and carrots may tempt a very sick horse to eat. Bran can be useful to help mix medicine, although it will have little feeding value. Alfalfa can be very tempting and is very nutritious. Cooked foods like boiled barley may tempt some horses, as may sugar beet. Sick horses need careful management to ensure that their digestive system continues to function efficiently.

Preparing sugar beet and bran mashes

Sugar beet – there are three main types:

- Cubes need to be soaked for 24 hours. There should be a ratio of 1 part cubes to 4 parts water. Once soaked, all sugar beet should be used within 12 hours. During hot weather especially, it can ferment very quickly and lead to colic.

- Shreds are soaked for 12 hours in a ratio of about 1 part shreds to 3 parts water. Many establishments prefer to use shreds because they cannot then be confused with horse and pony cubes.

- Speedi-beet can be soaked and be ready to eat within 10 minutes when using cold water. This can be very useful for the one horse owner.

Bran mashes

Although bran mashes are not fed as frequently as they used to be, they still have a use and may be required for a sick horse or to encourage the digestive system to keep functioning.

To prepare a bran mash you require a bucket, boiling water, bran, salt and something to cover the bucket (a hessian sack is best).

- Weigh out the amount of bran required – 2lb (1kg approximately) for a horse.

- Mix the bran and a tablespoon of salt together. Always do this before adding the water or you will end up with a large lump of salt, which will discourage the horse from eating.

- Pour on the boiling water and mix with a wooden spoon. There should be enough water to make the bran of a crumbly consistency.

- Cover the bucket and leave to cool until the temperature is such that the horse will want to eat it.

- Some people add succulents or a handful of oats to make the mash more appetising.

Feeding hay and alternatives

There are two main types of hay:

- Meadow hay comes from pasture fields that are allowed to grow so that a crop can be taken. The feeding value can vary greatly depending on the types of grass that are in the field.

- Seed hay comes from fields that have been sown specifically for hay. The grasses are selected so the feeding value tends generally to be higher than meadow hay. There are usually a majority of good quality grasses such as perennial rye grass and timothy. A crop tends to be taken for three years and then the field will be re-sown. Seed hay tends to be coarser than meadow hay. It is often used for competition horses.

Many people feed wet hay nowadays to reduce dust and fungal spores being taken in by the horse. There are several different ways that hay can be treated:

- Immersing it in a container for about 20 minutes. It should then be removed and drained. If it is to be fed in a haynet it should be put in the net and weighed before being put in the container. Do not leave the hay in the water for more than 20 minutes or the feed value can be washed away. Soaked hay can be very heavy and care must be taken when handling it so that the handler does not injure him or herself.

- Spraying it with a hosepipe. This can be done for a few minutes. Using this much water can be a problem, especially if the establishment has a water meter. Also, if the hay is not shaken up the water may not reach the middle of the wedges.

- Steaming it. Put the hay into a plastic sack and add some boiling water. Seal the top of the bag by tying it tightly and leave the steam to permeate through the hay. This can be very efficient, but care must be taken with the boiling water.

Many people choose to feed haylage today as an alternative to hay. Haylage is vacuum-packed forage that has been packed when it is still at about 50% wet matter. The grass ferments in the bale and maintains a higher feeding value than hay. Many horses will work quite hard on haylage alone, with no hard feed. The bales come in various sizes. The bigger the bale, the more economical it is, but a bale must be used up quite quickly once it is opened.

If bales are damaged then the haylage will be unusable and should be disposed of.

Silage is generally considered not suitable for feeding horses, as it has a higher wet matter content than haylage and can be more prone to botulism. There are cases of horses being successfully fed on silage, but it is not recommended because of the potential risk.

Grass nuts can be used as part of the roughage component of the diet and are useful in hot summers when there is little grass and limited hay supplies.

If hay is in short supply it is possible to supplement some of the ration with good quality oat straw. It does have a low feeding value and so the condition of the animals should be monitored carefully.

Making a feed chart

If there are a number of horses in a yard a feed chart of some kind is essential to ensure that each horse is fed the correct amount of the type of feed he requires. Any responsible member of staff who has been trained can then undertake feeding and no horse will be incorrectly fed.

The most common method of producing a chart is by using a black or white board on the feed room wall, upon which any changes can easily be made.

The chart needs to show the horses' names, how many times a day they are fed, the type of food and the amount. Any additional supplements should also be noted.

The total amount of feed a horse requires per day is largely dependent on his bodyweight. This can be approximated by using a weigh tape, experience (by looking at the horse's height and type) or, to be totally accurate, a weighbridge. A horse needs between 2% and 2.5% of his bodyweight in feed per day, depending on whether or not he is a good doer, and his age. The figures below are an approximation of the amount of food per day needed for various heights of horse/pony:

16hh – 30lb (13.5 kg)

15hh – 25lb (11.5 kg)

14hh – 20lb (9.0 kg)

13hh – 15lb (7.0 kg)

12hh – 12lb (5.5 kg)

This amount can then be divided between roughage and hard food depending on the work the horse/pony is doing, who is riding him, the time of year and the type of food being fed.

For grass to be included as part of this daily total it must be good quality. A horse in light work can probably manage on 100% roughage/bulk food, but may require some hard food in winter.

It is better to feed small, regular hard feeds. It is advisable to make each hard feed no more that 4lb (1.8 kg) in weight. Giving a horse small regular feeds will help to stop him becoming bored and more closely mimic trickle feeding, which is the natural way he eats in the wild.

Fittening

Fittening a horse is the process of ensuring that he is capable of undertaking the work required of him. At Stage 2 level you are expected to be able to discuss a fittening routine for a horse that works approximately one hour a day, six days a week.

Every horse will be slightly different and you need to take into consideration such factors as how long he has been out of work (how soft is his condition), how many times he has been fit before, his age and breed, and the time of year. To get a horse to this basic level of fitness you need to work on a six to eight week programme of exercise, with a week of preparation prior to the start.

During the preparation week the following should be considered:

- Does the tack still fit the horse? If he is overweight or under-muscled it may need adjustment. Make sure the tack is clean and in good condition. It may be useful to use a girth sleeve initially to help prevent girth galls.

- Has the stable been prepared? The loosebox should be clean and well ventilated. Bringing a horse that has been living out into a dusty environment can lead to coughs and colds. Shavings, paper or hemp bedding may be better than straw to help keep dust levels down.

- Does he need shoeing? If the horse has had his shoes removed then the farrier should be booked to shoe him before the start of the programme.

- Does he need worming? If the worming routine of the yard has not been kept up while he has been off work he may well need a faecal egg count and consequent worming.

- Are his inoculations up to date? Check whether or not he is due for a booster.

- Does he need tidying up? It is a good idea to start grooming him and, if required, trim him and pull his mane and tail.

- What has he been eating? If he has been out at grass it is useful to bring him in daily for a couple of hours to allow time to undertake all the tasks and give him a very small hard feed. This will re-introduce concentrates slowly and decrease the possibility of colic. If he is to be fed hay then it is a good idea to soak the hay initially to help prevent coughing.

- How out of condition is he? If he is very unfit it may be a good idea to harden the girth and saddle area of the skin with surgical spirit or salt water to help prevent galls. Soft skin is more prone to rubs and galls.

- Does he have any health conditions or previous injuries? The fittening programme will need to take any such issues into account to ensure that the horse thrives and does not deteriorate in any way.

Once the actual ridden programme starts it is better for the horse still to be able to spend several hours a day out in the field if at all possible. This horse is only being fittened for regular work and if he is to stand in his box for twenty-three hours a day he is more likely to have filled legs, digestive disorders, coughs, and be very unhappy.

Suggested basic fittening programme

This programme is based upon working the horse six days a week with one rest day.

Week 1

Walking exercise only. Start on day one with about 15 minutes walking and build up daily to approximately one hour by the end of the week. Walking on a sound, flat surface (e.g. the road) is best. Walking on the road helps to harden tendons and tone up muscle. An outdoor surface could be used for the first day or two, but after that the horse and rider will become bored! Walking on rutted going could damage tendons, ligaments and joints. Keep a watch out for rubbed areas and galls. Towards the end of week 1 the horse may be receiving up to 10% hard feed depending on his temperament and attitude. A ration of a prepared mix or cube is the best type of feed as the horse will be receiving a complete balanced diet.

Week 2

Walking exercise only. By the end of the second week the horse should be working for the total period of time he will be working every day. For this basic fittening programme it is likely to be approximately 1½ hours. Some work in walk up hills can be introduced towards the end of this week. This will make him work harder without putting any more stress on the front legs. He should not be made to sweat hard or become laboured in his breathing. He may still be on 10% hard food or a little more, if necessary.

Week 3

Trotting can be introduced this week. Introduce short trots of about one minute's duration several times during the work period. The trot should be a balanced, working trot. As the week progresses increase the length of each trot. Ensure you do not over-stress the horse. His breathing should not become laboured, nor should he sweat excessively. His hard feed may increase to 15% of his total food intake.

Week 4

During week 4 the length of the trot sessions will increase progressively. Towards the end of the week trotting up hill should be introduced. Work on grass, if not already introduced, can be started. The horse may still be on 15% concentrates, or may need a little more.

The time taken in the first four weeks will be of lasting benefit to the horse, hardening up muscles, tendons and ligaments. Many people find this time 'boring' and cut it short. For the long-term fitness and well-being of the horse two weeks of walking and two weeks of trotting should always be the rule.

Roadwork is often an important part of developing a horse's fitness. Exercising in pairs keeps horses content and confident.

Week 5

Canter work can be introduced this week in the same way as the trot was introduced in Week 3. The horse may, however, now be starting to feel 'well' and cantering should be introduced with caution. A good surface is essential and, if it is in the country, riding next to a hedge line will help with control. Easing the horse into canter from a trot should ensure there are no 'fireworks'. As the week progresses the length and frequency of each canter can be increased gradually. Lungeing could be introduced this week, as could short periods of schooling using big school figures and trotting poles. The horse may still be on 15% concentrates.

Week 6

The length of the canters will continue to be increased, and some hill work in canter can be introduced towards the end of the week. Schooling can become a little more intense, and jumping introduced over small show jumps and natural obstacles outside. At the end of the week a small dressage competition could be attended if the horse is being readied for a horse trials competition. He may now be receiving approximately 20% concentrates.

Week 7

The work will continue as per Week 6. The canters may get a little longer and faster if required and, if the horse does not feel fit enough, the tempo of the rest of the work can be increased as well. Towards the end of Week 7 the horse could have a pipe-opener (a short half-gallop) to assess his fitness by monitoring his recovery rate and also to help open up the lungs. The horse could be taken to a show jumping competition and/or cross-country schooling. His level of concentrate food may well still be at 20% or he may require a little more.

Week 8

If the work undertaken in Week 7 showed the horse was at the level of fitness required, then Week 8 can be a refining week with the flatwork and jumping being improved. If he is not yet fit enough then the intensity of the work needs to be upped a little. This should help him achieve the fitness level required. His level of concentrate feed should

A pipe-opener will help to assess a horse's level of fitness.

only go up if he is not managing to cope with the work level required. The work level should stay ahead of hard feed levels to ensure digestive disorders (such as colic and azoturia), filled legs and poor behaviour do not ensue. Many people feed too much concentrate feed and not enough quality bulk food. If the horse works well, without losing condition, on a small amount of hard feed it is not necessary to feed him any more. The more bulk the horse has in his daily intake, the better his digestive health will be and the less bored he will become.

At all times during a fittening programme it is important to monitor the horse carefully.

The change in routine, feed and potential stress can lead to the horse showing signs of coughs and colds. Possible contact with different horses can also lead to health issues.

When getting a horse fit and when exercising a fit horse it is important to be aware of possible leg injuries the horse may receive. Concussion injuries can be caused by riding on hard ground, riding too fast on poor going or hard conditions, and trotting fast and in an unbalanced way on roads. Working a horse in heavy ground or on uneven going, before his legs are fit to cope, can lead to strain injuries. Jumping on deep or uneven going, riding downhill at speed, poor riding unbalancing the horse and too much work when not fit enough, can also lead to strains.

Cooling off after work

It is important that a horse is cooled off after work so his metabolism has the chance to return to normal. This will assist in him remaining healthy and not catching a chill. Once work has finished the horse should be walked around and allowed to stretch. This may be mounted or in hand. If it is safe to do so the girth can be loosened a hole. Depending on the weather, a light rug may need to be put on the horse. Once he has cooled down, dried off and has stopped blowing he can be offered a small amount of water and be washed down. If it is cold, warm water should be used. (In very cold weather it is better not to wash the horse down, just to brush off the sweat marks when he is dry.) He can then be dried off and walked around again if necessary. Water can be offered again. He can then be allowed to graze, or be given a haynet. His legs need to be checked for injury. Small amounts of water can be offered at regular intervals until he is not thirsty any more. Check that the horse is eating his food as normal. A horse that is eating well is usually healthy and not stressed.

The day after hard work the legs should be checked for injury again and the horse trotted up to test for lameness.

Roughing off

Roughing off is the process whereby a fit horse is readied to be turned out for a break. Hunters are usually roughed off at the end of the hunting season and eventers may be roughed off at the end of their season.

The process takes about 10 to 14 days depending on the time of year and how much the horse is to be let down fitness-wise.

- The amount of work the horse undertakes is cut down over the days, both in intensity and length of time.

- The amount of time he spends in the stable is reduced, i.e. he spends more time in the field daily.

- If the horse is wearing more than one rug, the number of rugs he wears is gradually reduced.

- As the workload decreases so the amount of hard feed should decrease.

- Grooming should be cut down to a minimum so the natural oils in the horse's coat can build up. Allow the mane and tail to grow.

- A decision needs to be taken as to whether the horse's shoes are removed or left on. If a horse has brittle feet then it may be better to leave the shoes on. If the break is for a long period and it will allow for decent foot growth then the quality of the horn may improve with no nails through it.

- Choose a pleasant day weatherwise to turn him out finally. He may wear a New Zealand rug all the time if it is winter.

- Do not forget about the roughed-off horse. He still needs to be checked daily. If it is winter some people turn the horse out during the day and bring him in at night. Often, in this case, concentrates are still fed so that the horse does not lose all his condition.

What the assessor is looking for

- Knowledge of feeding and watering the horse is one of the most basic and essential areas of horsemastership. It is therefore important that you are able to describe clearly and with good understanding, the knowledge underpinning this subject.

- In the wild, the horse will access water at will. Stabled (and, to a degree, at grass) the horse needs you to provide for him. A clean, fresh source is the first priority, then clean utensils and regular renewal (for the stabled horse). You should be aware of the horse's intake on a daily basis so that you can recognise any changes that might indicate a problem in health. Care when offering water to a hot or tired horse is important. Horses should have constant access to water but it is preferable that they do not imbibe a large amount immediately after eating their concentrate ration.

- You need to show that you understand the most common ways of providing water. You must be able to discuss the pros and cons of these methods, both in the stable and in the field. If you draw on your practical experience this will show in the discussion and be positive.

- You should be able to discuss the basic rules by which feeding the horse is governed. Consider each of these 'rules' and make sure that you can give a clear reason to support each one. Be able to pick up on any of these rules in any order, as this is how you are likely to be in the group theory section of your exam. Get into the habit of recalling each of the rules at random, then if seven or eight rules have already been given, you will be able to recall the elusive one or two that have not been mentioned.

- You are likely to be offered feed samples to look at. Often these are contained in glass jars and the samples may have been there quite a long time! If this is the case, the smell and appearance of the feed may not be as fresh as you would choose for your horse. Be able to recognise the feed and give a brief description of when and for what sort of horse the food might be used. Learn which feeds have a 'heating effect' on a horse (e.g. oats and maize). Learn which feeds have a fattening effect. Know which feeds are considered suitable for horses doing fast work.

- You will be asked to assess the quality of feed samples. In Stage 1 you had to identify a variety of feed samples. Make sure you can still do this if you are not regularly involved in feeding different feedstuffs. Oats and barley are most frequently confused. Oats are longer and thinner than barley; the latter's seeds are plumper and shorter.

- Feeding horses and ponies that live at grass and are required to work from grass needs some consideration, and the assessor will seek this knowledge. Be aware of the bulk requirement for these animals, particularly when the nutritional quality of the grass is low in winter.

- Know about feeding old and sick horses, which again need specialist consideration. Old horses need to be kept warm and maintain their body weight to assist this. They may also suffer from deterioration of their grinding teeth (molars) and so the bulk ration may need careful thought. Sick horses need to be tempted to eat to maintain strength and may need easily digested feeds or feeds which do not require much 'effort' to eat.

- You may be asked about the preparation of certain feeds. Sugar beet is a valuable feed but needs care in preparation and management or it can ferment and cause problems. Know the difference between sugar beet shreds and cubes and the length of time each needs to be soaked. Bran mashes were used extensively for many types of working horse until the huge development of knowledge in the horse's digestion of food and the nutritional content of feeds. Bran mashes are now used less frequently, but it is still important that you have a knowledge of the use of bran, know how to make a bran mash and understand where it has an application in the modern management of horses.

- You will be asked about the feeding of hay as a bulk ration, when and why it might need to be soaked, and how this would be done. You will also be asked about feeding alternatives to hay.

- You should be able to discuss the structure of a simple feed chart and why it is important to have one on a yard.

- By the time you are competent at Stage 2 level, you should be familiar with seeing, and hopefully being involved with, the fittening work of horses in your care. You must be able to describe clearly the gradual process by which a horse in 'soft' condition (i.e. one that has not been in regular work for some time) is developed in both exercise and feeding to become a horse that is capable of regular work.

- You will be expected to describe the value of an increasing period of walking exercise, then the introduction of trot, and from this the gradual development of canter to further the fitness process.

- You should understand the influences that affect the time it would take to develop fitness. These would include how long the horse has been out of work, what sort of type or breeding he is, how fat he is when you start, what facilities you have to develop the fitness work.

- You must be aware that horses brought into a stable having lived at grass, may be susceptible to coughs or colds because of the change in environment. You should have ideas as to how this risk can be minimised.

- You will be expected to discuss the potential risk of the horse developing sores, or 'galls', where skin contact is made with tack when the horse is unused to wearing equipment. Know the precautions you would take to minimise this, such as careful management of the tack to keep it supple and comfortable, the use of soft numnahs and girths, and taking great care with the fitting of tack to fat, unfit horses.

- You will be asked about the gradual development of the horse's feed ration in relation to the increase of work, bearing in mind that the field-kept horse's diet is likely to have been exclusively grass. You must be able to describe how you would gradually introduce hard food, and some kind of bulk ration such as hay or haylage as the horse becomes stabled for longer periods.

- You should have some knowledge of feeds which would be appropriate to the gradual development of a fitter horse. You may be asked to recognise feed samples.

- The reverse process of fittening is 'roughing off'. You are likely to be asked about this procedure, and you should recognise that the roughing-off programme can be achieved in a considerably shorter period of time than the building up of fitness. Be able to discuss the effects of weather, time of year, type of horse and facilities available in the planning of a roughing-off programme.

- You may be asked about the possible risk of injury when getting a horse fitter. Roadwork carries risks of subjecting the horse to concussion, which may result in an injury such as a splint. Working a horse in heavy ground or uneven going, before his limbs are fit enough to cope, can leave him at risk of strain injuries to muscles, tendons or ligaments.

- The gradual cooling off of the horse after a period of work, especially when he has exerted himself to the point of sweating, is important, as is the general care of the horse after work. Make sure you can discuss clearly a system for bringing the horse back to his stable, having walked him to the point of him being cool, dried off and not blowing. This would include loosening the girth and throwing a light rug or anti-sweat sheet over him to prevent him becoming chilled.

How to become competent

- Feeding is an art, but as with any art you must learn the theory behind the practice. Learn the rules for feeding and watering so that they come automatically to mind. Familiarise yourself with as many different types of feed samples as you can.

- Study the feed chart in your yard; discuss which horses have what rations and why, with the stable manager or your instructor.

- Take an interest in the horses that you ride and what feed they are given. In due course you will then learn to adjust the feed ration according to how the horse looks (if he needs to put weight on or is too fat then the feed may need adjusting). You will realise that the way the horse 'feels' when you ride him may be affected by what feed he is eating.

- Become interested in the different prepared feeds that are on the market these days. Most feed companies provide extensive literature on all their products; collect this paperwork and read it. It can give you background information on the nutrients available in each feed and this will help you in due course when this information is required from you at Stage 3.

- Consider how horses are fed both at grass and in the stable. In winter, grass-kept horses need care with regard to noticing their condition and monitoring how much they are fed, particularly when the weather is freezing and if snow falls.

- It is important not only that you read up about how to develop fitness in the horse, but also that you experience it by actually doing it.

- Be able to recognise the horse that is in 'soft' condition – what he looks like, what he 'feels' like – both when you groom him and apply his tack.

- Learn to recognise what the horse 'feels' like when you first ride him after a period of being out of work. This 'feel' should then follow through as the horse begins to develop fitness. He will find his work easier, he will sweat less, he will start to lose his flab and fat and become more muscled and streamlined in his physique.

- Recognise the difference in the horse in the stable – he will look different as he loses weight and becomes more toned in his muscles. He may change a little in character as he feels more 'full of himself' – he may nip when his girth is tightened, as his rugs are applied or when he is groomed.

- Look at different horses in your yard and find out what work they are doing; then look at their build and physique, feel their condition in terms of their coat and muscular tone and firmness. The legs of a horse that is developing fitness and of a fit horse in regular work, should be cool, firm and not showing any heat or puffiness. A horse in work may have his mane and tail tidied, and in winter may be clipped.

- In the unfortunate event that a horse does develop any type of injury during the fittening process, make sure that you look at the injury and then discuss the cause and subsequent treatment and management with your instructor or stable manager.

The Principles of Stabling and Grassland Care for Horses

5 Credits

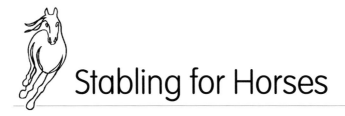

Stabling for Horses

The candidate should know:

The requirements for stable design and construction

About horse behaviour and welfare when stabled

The requirements for grassland care and pasture maintenance

About horse behaviour and welfare at grass

Stable sizes vary greatly according to whether they have been custom made (in which case they may vary from around 10ft by 10ft (3m by 3m), which could be suitable for a pony, to 12ft by 14ft (3.6m by 4.2m) or bigger, which would be more appropriate for a horse) or they have been converted from existing farm buildings, in which case they may be much larger (or occasionally smaller!).

- Stables are usually either of a traditional or American barn system. The advantages of an American barn are that it is easier for staff to work as everything is under one roof and enclosed from the elements. Security can be better, horses can be more easily observed and the environment can be warmer in winter. For the horses, though, it can be boring as they are often unable to see outdoors. If the passageway down the middle of the barn is not wide enough then horses can be intimidated and even bitten by others as they go past. If the partitioning between boxes is not strong enough then horses can be threatened by their neighbours. Disease can travel more easily between horses, especially if the ventilation is not good.

*An 'American barn-type' stable yard. Stables open onto a covered
yard area with an entrance at one or preferably both ends.*

Construction

Stable walls can be built of various materials.

- Brick is ideal because it is fireproof, long-lasting and is warm in winter and cool in summer. Unfortunately it is a very expensive way to build stables and can take a long time to construct.

- Wooden stables are very popular because they are cheaper and, as long as the base has been prepared, they can be constructed in a day. Wooden stables can be a fire hazard and they need to be regularly maintained. Horses can kick and chew through them. They can be cold in winter and hot in summer.

- Breeze blocks are cheaper than house bricks and are fireproof. They take longer

125

to construct than wooden stables and do not always look aesthetically pleasing. They can be cold in winter as they are hollow in the middle.

- Corrugated iron is not a good material to use for stable walls. It has edges that, over time, become more defined and on which a horse can injure himself. It is not very strong and could be kicked right through, leaving a horse with a severely injured leg. It is also very hot in summer and very cold in winter as there is no insulation.

The stable roof needs to be high enough so that a horse will not hit his head. A height of about 12ft (3.6m) to the eaves, with a pitched roof, should be adequate.

Stable roofs can also be made of a variety of materials.

- A tiled roof is ideal but is very expensive and needs to be well maintained so that tiles do not fall on humans or horses.

- Many wooden stables have wooden roofs that are covered in roofing felt of some kind. This is waterproof, but does require careful maintenance because, over time, the felt can be ripped by the wind. The stables themselves are usually very dark as there is no natural light coming through the roof.

- Corrugated iron does not make a good roof as it is very noisy when it rains and lacks insulation. If it is put over a wooden roof then it is more acceptable.

- Onduline is a product that is similar to corrugated iron, but is coated with a substance to help insulate it. This works well as a roof and also plastic sheeting can be inserted into the roof to give some natural light.

If the roof is wider than the stable to provide an overhang this makes a huge difference to the horse and the keeper. They can stay dry and warm more easily.

It is important for a stable to have guttering both front and back to collect rain and take it

A well-constructed wooden loosebox with an overhang.

*Louvre boards
providing extra
ventilation in a
wooden loosebox.*

to drains or water butts via downpipes that are situated so that a horse cannot chew them.

Good ventilation is vital in a stable. There are a variety of ways this can be provided. Within an American barn system it is more difficult to ensure a free flow of air without there being a huge through-draught.

In a traditional stable set-up it is better to have a window on the same side as the door and the top of the window opening inward. This will stop a through-draught and direct the air up into the roof of the stable. The top door of a stable is usually left open and this will help provide good ventilation. Windows must be protected with a metal grid so that the horse cannot break the glass.

Louvre boards are often set in the eaves at either end of a wooden stable block. These are overlapping boards which face upwards to help stop rain and snow penetrating. They are a good way to help keep air flowing without causing a draught on the horses' backs. Air bricks (bricks with holes in) serve the same purpose but are not quite so efficient.

Some stables have 'draw chimneys' on the ridges of roofs. These draw the air up out of the top of them and ensure circulation.

Stable doors should be wide enough for horse and handler to get through safely. A width of 4ft 6in (137cm) is the generally accepted norm. For ponies 4ft (120cm) may be adequate. The bottom door should be high enough so that it protects the horse from the elements but also discourages him from jumping over. A height of about 5ft (152cm) is suitable for a horse but a smaller height is better for a pony so he can put his head over the door comfortably.

The top door should be securely fixed back so there is no possibility of the wind catching it and blowing it shut on the horse's face. The height to the top of a doorway should be a minimum of 10ft (3m). A metal anti-chewing strip along the top of the bottom door is a good idea to discourage the horse from chewing. The top bolt should be of the traditional stable bolt type as this is more difficult for the horse to undo but, if he does learn this trick, a clip can be applied to rectify this. There should always be a second, bottom bolt for security. A kick bolt is best for this as staff do not have to bend down to undo it. Some horses have an anti-weave device attached to the door. There are two types – one that stops the horse from putting its head over the door, and another that is V-shaped and allows the horse to put his head out but restricts sideways movement.

Doors should open outwards. If they open inwards there is the possibility of hitting the horse and, if he is cast, you may not be able to get in to help him.

Stables should be built so that the doors do not face the prevailing wind. If they face north or east the top doors may have to be shut during the winter when snow falls.

An anti-weave grille which allows the horse to put his head out and look round the yard.

Sliding doors are often found in American barn systems as they do not block the central passageway when opened. They are usually heavier than traditional doors and slide on rails at the top – and, sometimes, the bottom – of the entrance. There are different types of locking mechanisms, some of which automatically 'click' shut when fully closed. Such locking devices must always be checked carefully to ensure security. These types of door need regular maintenance or they can become heavy and difficult to open.

Nowadays stable floors tend to be made of concrete, a material that is fairly cheap and durable. It should have a 'brush' finish, i.e. before it is completely set a stiff brush is passed over the surface to roughen it up. This stops it from becoming slippery. With a concrete floor, the horse's bed needs to be deep or to have rubber matting put over the top, otherwise it can be cold and hard to stand on. Rubber matting should never be used without any bedding.

The floor should always slope very slightly downwards to the back of the stable, with a drainage channel running all the way along the back wall. In the middle there should be a drainage hole. The floor should never slope to the front of the stable. The horse spends a great deal of time standing at the front of the box, and if the urine drains to the front he will be standing in this. Also the urine will run onto the yard making it unsightly and unhealthy.

Floors can also simply be made of packed earth. These do, however, require first-class maintenance as they can become wet and dirty and over time can wear away making the stable floor uneven.

Stable bricks (traditionally of a bluish colour) were historically used for stable floors. These can still be seen in some old yards. They form an excellent floor, but nowadays it is not financially viable to use bricks.

There should be a minimum of stable fittings. The more there are in the stable, the more likely the horse is to injure himself.

There needs to be a tying-up ring. This should be at a height of about 5ft (152cm). It is better placed on the side wall nearer to the door. The horse can then be tied up and the person working with him does not have to keep going near his hind legs. There should be a piece of string attached to the ring so the horse is not attached directly to the ring. It is no use using plastic baler twine for this unless it has been weakened. (If sisal baler twine is not available then plastic baler twine can be unravelled and half of the width used.) Full-strength normal plastic baler twine is so strong that it will not break if a horse struggles.

A second tie ring for a haynet is often found on the same wall as the tying-up ring. This should be at a minimum height of about 6ft 6in (198cm). This means that staff will be able to reach to hang up the net, but the empty net should not be hanging low enough for the horse to get his foot caught in it. Some yards do not like haynets and prefer to feed hay from the floor. This is the safest way to feed hay, but can be wasteful. High hayracks are popular in some places, but they can take up a lot of space within the loosebox, and the horse can get hay seeds dropping into his eye.

Some people have a fixture on the wall for a mineral lick of some sort. As long as a lick is kept in the bracket there is little danger of injury. An empty bracket can be a potential hazard for the horse. After a few years the mineral lick can rust the bracket and it may come loose. It then needs to be replaced or taken out altogether.

A permanent feed manger in a loosebox can take up a lot of room and so be a potential danger. It is more natural for the horse to be fed on the floor with a feed bucket that can be removed once he has finished eating. If the horse is a messy eater, however, this can lead to waste and encourage vermin so a permanent corner manger may be used. This is usually fixed at breast height. If it has a removable bowl, the metal bracket should have the facility to close away so the horse cannot catch himself on it.

In a loosebox water can be provided in two main ways – by bucket or automatic waterer. These systems are discussed on page 102.

There needs to be a source of electric light within the box. A strip light high in the ceiling with a protective outer casing is popular as it provides light over a large area. All lighting should be enclosed so that the horse cannot break the bulb, with obvious potential consequences. The light switch should be outside the stable and out of reach of the horse, as should the wiring. If the wiring has to be positioned in such a place that a horse may be able to chew it, then it must be enclosed.

Always work on the premise that there should be as few fittings in the stable as possible.

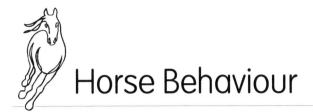

Horse Behaviour

Behaviour and lifestyle

This is part of the theory section of the exam where you will be sitting in a group with the assessor. The assessors will also, however, look at how you work with any of the horses you come into contact with on the day.

For Stage 1 you learned about the horse's natural lifestyle. Being a herd animal that grazes, establishes a pecking order and enjoys living with others, having frequent physical contact with them is the basis of the horse's natural way of life. We must remember that by putting horses in stables we are turning this lifestyle upside down because we take away the freedom to move, eat and interact with other horses as and when they want to. Some horses may develop repetitive habits to compensate for their lack of freedom; others may have no issues at all. Some can be unhappy and their behaviour may become difficult to manage. Consequently it is important to be able to read a horse's body language.

A horse's ears can tell you many things:

- If they are pricked strongly forward then something has caught the horse's attention and he is focusing on it. If they are forward and relaxed then he is interested in what is around him but happy and does not feel threatened. If the ears are flat back then the horse feels under pressure and is ready to protect himself. If one ear is forward and one back then he is feeling relaxed about life.

Examples of horse's ears giving away the way he feels.

The horse's eyes will give you similar messages:

- A kind, gentle eye that looks big and soft will mean the horse is feeling well disposed to his surroundings and those around him. A staring, focused eye will mean that the horse is in a heightened sense of awareness and may well be prepared to protect himself, either by running or preparing to defend himself. His nostrils may well be flared at the same time and he may be snorting.

A horse's tail can also tell you something about its owner. A relaxed tail indicates a relaxed horse. A constantly twitching tail and/or a tail held high can betray a heightened sense of agitation. A tail clamped down may indicate a horse about to kick.

A happy, contented horse will be calm and unconcerned, both in his stable and in the field. A worried, tense horse will be agitated, unable to keep still. He may sweat and frequently pass droppings.

These signs are just as true whether the horse is in a stable, in a field or being ridden. If he is in a field and is frightened by something, his immediate reaction will be to run away from the object of his fear and, when he feels he is a safe distance away, turn and look at the 'dragon', snort and be ready to run again. If he is being ridden this can create an issue as he will still want to run away at speed from the object! The better he is schooled, the more he will take notice of the rider's leadership, and focus on his work instead of the object of fear.

In the stable a frightened horse cannot run. In this situation he will prepare to fight, either putting his head in the corner and his hind legs into the middle of the box ready to kick, or he will attack with his teeth and front legs. Neither is acceptable behaviour within a stabled environment and the horse must learn to trust those around him. When he feels safe he will not display this behaviour. In the meantime those looking after him must show patience, discipline, authority and consistent behaviour.

In the summer months horses who are turned out during the day may well be annoyed by flies and biting insects. They may also not like the heat and so become unsettled. Changing the routine and putting the horses out at night and in during the day can help to alleviate these issues.

If the ground becomes hard and the grass sparse, unshod horses may show signs of being footsore and may become fractious because there is little to eat and occupy them.

If there are mares and geldings together in the same field, mares coming into season can upset the geldings. The latter may feel they are still stallions and fight each other for the attention of the mares. It is better to keep mares and geldings in separate paddocks to limit this type of behaviour.

Safe handling

The way in which a horse is handled can have a huge affect on his well-being. A horse needs to learn to trust those around him, then he will become relaxed. The person/people looking after him need to be consistent in their behaviour and, as far as possible, set up a regular routine. Fair treatment and consistent discipline are essential for the horse to become settled and learn to trust those around him. When handling an unknown horse it is sensible to wear a riding hat, and safe footwear is necessary. When leading any horse gloves are essential as they will protect against rope burns.

If you are unsure how a horse will behave when he comes out of the stable it is a good idea to put on a bridle rather than a headcollar for greater control. A cavesson and lunge line can give you more control than a headcollar, but probably not as much as a bridle. Using a lunge line with a headcollar or bridle can give you more leeway for control, as long as you are used to handling one. If you are not, then it is easy to get the line tangled up in your hand, or even trip over it. If there is a particularly difficult horse to lead then you might consider using a Chifney (an anti-rearing bit).

New, difficult, young and untrained horses must always be dealt with by a confident and competent person. A nervous person will usually make the horse anxious. A handler lacking in confidence will usually not be positive enough to ensure that the horse receives discipline or reward in the correct amount and at the right time.

It must be remembered there can be a difference in the way a person handles their own horse and ones they do not know. This is why it is important to show safe

A Chifney bit should only be used when supervision by an experienced person is available.

techniques when handling horses in an exam. A private owner may take 'small liberties' with their own horse, but it would not be possible or advisable to do the same with a horse you do not know. Always talking to a horse before going into the stable is a simple example. Your own horse may not be startled by you going into his box, but a horse that has not built up a relationship with humans needs to know his space is about to be invaded and get into the habit of moving back from the doorway when somebody enters his stable. Always tying the horse up and going to his front before doing anything at the hindquarters are very important factors to help improve your own personal safety. These details are often criticised as unnecessary by some taking BHS exams, but for personal safety in any yard environment they need to be an automatic part of a horse handler's behaviour.

Accommodating a new horse

When bringing a new horse onto a yard it is always best if he can be put in an isolation yard for about two weeks to ensure he has no issues that can be passed on to others in the yard. If possible he should be able to see other, sensible horses. He should have ad lib access to bulk, as eating can keep him occupied and help him to settle. Putting on stable bandages or brushing boots can help protect the legs until the horse is less likely to be restless within the loosebox. Making just one person responsible for the horse will help the newcomer to build up a relationship and a routine more quickly. If the facility to isolate the horse is not available then he should be put next to a sensible horse on the yard. When turning the horse out for the first time he should be put in a field either by himself or with one quiet, sensible horse. The number of horses he is turned out with can be built up slowly so that the pecking order can be established without too much argument and therefore less likelihood of injury.

Difficult to catch

Catching a horse that does not want to be caught can be a real trial. If a horse does not go out in the field very often he may just want to stay out so he can enjoy himself in his natural environment. Turning him out more frequently can help to overcome the issue. Making sure that there is a positive reason for him to go back to his box (like a feed), rather than always being caught to be ridden, is another way to help catch him. If he has had a bad experience in the past – for example, he has been caught and then chastised for some reason – this may make him think the same thing is going to happen again. Overcoming this problem can take a lot of time and patience. Turning the horse out in a well-fitting leather headcollar can assist in catching him to help move the process forward and start to restore the horse's trust in you.

Anti-social behaviour in the ridden horse

Sometimes when a horse is being ridden in the company of others, he can appear bad-tempered. He may put his ears back, adopt a threatening body posture or try to kick out. This is often because he feels threatened by the other horses and is trying to protect himself before he is 'attacked' by them. He may feel that the others are invading his 'personal space'. Being ridden means that he is unable to sort out the pecking order naturally and so resorts to this kind of anti-social behaviour. Making sure that horses have enough space when being ridden, slowly building up their confidence to work with others and positive riding will help to overcome this.

Ill-fitting tack

If a horse's tack does not fit he can show this in several ways. A stoic horse may just try to carry on and not show any behavioural change, but ill-fitting tack will usually mean that the horse is at the least uncomfortable and at the worst in considerable pain.

If the saddle is the issue the horse may not stand still to be mounted, he may dip his back as the rider tries to get on, and may then explode into bucking, trying to get rid of the pain once the rider is on board. He may refuse to go forward or even appear lame.

If it is the bridle that is causing pain the horse may not want the bit put in his mouth, he may shake his head frequently, he may try to find different ways of evading the contact, or he may refuse to go forward or try to rush off.

If a horse shows signs of bad behaviour when being ridden or when being prepared to be ridden, always look into the possibility of him being in pain from the tack before considering anything else.

Grassland Care

Assessors may have a chart showing poisonous plants that you may be asked to name, or they might bring in some actual examples.

You must be able to discuss the ideal field suitable for horses. Remember you are discussing the *ideal* field, and this is often not achieved. Horses frequently live safely and thrive in compromised environments that are safe and adequate.

The following are points you should consider for your ideal field:

- The acreage should be acceptable for the number of horses using the field for grazing. It is generally accepted that you should allow 2 acres (0.8ha) for the first horse and 1 acre (0.4ha) for each horse thereafter.

- The ideal fencing is post and rail with a hedge behind it. This gives security and a certain amount of protection from the elements.

- A self-filling water trough positioned away from the entrance to the field and away from overhanging trees.

- A secure gate that opens easily. The gateway may have hardcore put down to

Poisonous plants.

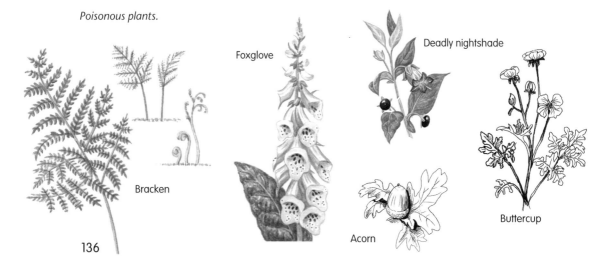

Bracken

Foxglove

Deadly nightshade

Acorn

Buttercup

stop it becoming too muddy during winter. The gate must be wide enough to allow tractor access so that any necessary work can be undertaken.

- A field shelter in good repair or other form of wind-break/shelter to keep the worst of the elements from the horses. Remember: a field shelter should be three-sided so that a horse can escape if others attack him.

- Adequate grazing or hay/haylage must be available at all times.

- There should be no poisonous plants.

- The underlying soil should be free draining to avoid excess mud.

- The field should be free from hazards.

- The field is flat or with a slight slope.

Quality grazing has a variety of good grasses that have a good growth at the bottom near the ground and so produce a dense sward. Perennial rye grass and some of the fescues are examples of this.

To ensure grazing is maintained to a high standard it is important not to overgraze the pasture and to make sure it is rested regularly. Cross-grazing with sheep or cattle (if the fencing allows this and there is enough land) will help to keep the pasture even and reduce the worm burden. Weeds should be dug up or sprayed. If sprayed, horses should be kept off the land for the time recommended by the manufacturers of the herbicide used. Poisonous plants should be removed and burnt. You should be able to recognise the most common poisonous plants: ragwort, foxglove, deadly nightshade, laburnum, bracken, yew, hemlock, buttercup and acorns are some of those frequently found.

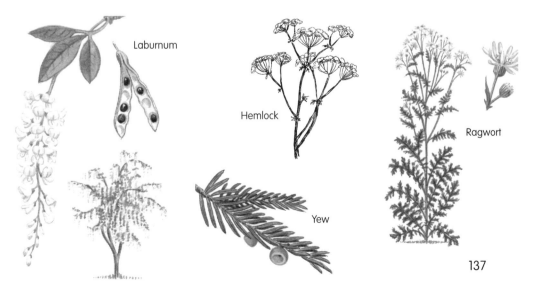

Laburnum

Hemlock

Ragwort

Yew

137

A soil analysis is useful as the land can then be fertilised as per its requirements. Fertiliser is usually applied in spring. Again horses should be kept from the land until the fertiliser is well washed in. Some fertilisers are better applied in the autumn, but advice needs to be taken about this.

In the spring the land should be harrowed and rolled to help encourage sward growth and to level and compress the surface. Any poached areas should be reseeded, although for long-term benefit horses should not graze a reseeded area for a few months until the grass is established.

Fences, gates and water troughs should be kept in good repair for the safety and welfare of the horses.

Post and rail fence and a well-hung, secure gate would offer a safe environment for horses in this field.

Barbed-wire fence and damaged gate would offer potential danger to horses in the field.

Droppings should be picked up daily, but if the field is large or there is not the manpower to do this then the droppings should be harrowed regularly during dry weather in the summer to help kill the worm burden and assist the uptake of the manure into the ground.

If long grasses or 'roughs' (areas where the horses dung and so do not graze) appear they should be topped to encourage good grasses to grow.

If there are ditches around the boundary these should be dug out regularly as this can really help in keeping the field well drained.

Those with enough land keep one field for winter turnout to ensure the others are not wrecked and so come into the spring in good condition.

What the assessor is looking for

- You may be standing either in the stable yard or in a stable itself when the assessor asks about the structure. For example against an ideal picture, describe the suitability of the facilities around you.

- Look at the height of the roof to the eaves. The eaves should be high enough so that if the horse tosses his head in the air he will not knock his head. Many converted stables have supporting beams for the roof that are too low.

- You should be able to look at all aspects of the stable you are discussing and show that you recognise the elements that are safe for a horse's welfare.

- Be positive with your comments but not too dogmatic.

- Be prepared to give reasons for liking or disliking some aspects of the construction.

- Make sure you are interested in what the other candidates are saying so you can add further comments if necessary.

- Do not lean against the stable wall.

- The assessor is looking for you to show that you have practical knowledge in dealing with different types of horses. You must show that you recognise the importance of building up a rapport with the horses you are responsible for. You should be able to discuss the safe handling of different types of horses in the field, in the stable and when being ridden. Common sense is important here, both on the theoretical side and in practical situations.

- Be able to describe the horse's natural lifestyle and discuss how stabling him changes and disturbs this.

- You must be able to describe signs that indicate nervousness in the horse in a stabled situation, at grass, and out and about while being ridden. At grass, the horse can demonstrate his instinctive reaction, which is to run away from, then turn to look at, something he fears. In the stable he cannot run so he turns his hindquarters towards the perceived danger and 'threatens' with his hind legs. When ridden, the horse may choose the option to buck to try to dislodge something on his back of which he is afraid.

- Be aware that horses can be dangerous if not handled with knowledge, care and authority.

- Know how you would integrate a new horse into your yard if he had never been there before.

- You may be asked to discuss the behaviour you might see in a horse that is usually stabled when he is turned out in the field and is then difficult to catch. Such behaviour may stem from anxiety if the horse is not used to being free in the field, but it is more likely to be associated with the horse's desire to stay free in an environment which he prefers.

- Be able to discuss and recognise anti-social behaviour in the horse when being ridden. Traits you might be expected to discuss may include the horse being bad-tempered, laying his ears back at other horses close to him, and threatening them with his heels and/or teeth if they come too close behind him or beside him.

- You may be asked to describe how a horse might behave if his tack does not fit. Very simply, the horse is likely to be uncomfortable and even in pain, and any behavioural traits showing resistance will reflect this.

- You must be able to describe what you consider to be the 'ideal' field for a horse(s) to live in. The main points of discussion you should be able to elaborate on a little would be: size of field relative to the number of horses, condition of grass, availability of water supply and shelter, gate access, and type of fencing.

- Having described what you consider to be good quality grazing you must then know what is essential to sustain and promote the quality of the grass.

- You should be able to recognise and describe the most common poisonous plants indigenous to British horse pastures or surrounding environments.

How to become competent

- Be observant and ask questions. Study any and every stable yard you have the opportunity to visit, even if it is just two stables in the back garden of a friend's house. Ask questions as to how efficient the stables are for the care and comfort of the horses.

- Look at the materials from which stables are built, particularly in older stable yards where the buildings have stood the test of time.

- Ask how cool the stables are in summer and how warm in winter.

- Look at the flooring under the bedding. See whether there are drains or whether the floor is sloping (to the back or the front?). Is the floor concrete? If so, is it ridged or brush-finished for anti-slip? Are there old-fashioned stable bricks?

- What fittings can you see? Lights, mangers, automatic-water devices, tie rings, racks?

- Look at the doors and windows.

- How does the overall yard layout strike you? Take in all the convenient aspects of the set-up (e.g. consider that an overhang on outside stables keeps an area dry to work in but may also cause drips where it ends!).

- Read about stable construction and design.

- The best way to prepare for this section is to be very 'hands on' and aware of the horses around you. You will achieve competence by observing and handling lots of horses in different situations.

- Never miss an opportunity to 'learn' about the horses you deal with. Never take them for granted and think you know them so well that you don't need to handle them with care and good practice. Horses react unpredictably to different conditions: weather, noise and unexpected activity can all affect the 'normal' behaviour of a horse. If you fail to regard these factors then sooner or later a horse will accidentally hurt you.

- Watch more experienced people manage young horses, stallions and perhaps spoilt horses that have come into your establishment for reschooling. Sometimes horses need to be reminded 'who is the boss'; they may need a short, sharp lesson in good manners. Horses learn through repetition and if they have been allowed to be unruly and rude, then they will continue to behave in this manner.

- Watch the way horses react and interact in the field and stable. Learn to 'read' the horse and be able to understand the way he is thinking – this will be the key to your competence as a horsemaster. You will then learn when to be firm and when to be sympathetic; you will know when the horse is being a 'brat' and when he is genuinely frightened and needs your reassurance. His confidence will then build from your competence.

- Always follow safe, practical procedures. Don't take risks, and don't take horses for granted, assuming that they will always behave in a predictable way.

- If taking Stage 2, you should be involved in some regular care of horses/ponies living and working from grass as well as caring for stabled horses. Make sure that you take responsibility for regularly checking the field in which these animals live for the maintenance of the basic facilities on which they rely.

- Be aware of the condition and maintenance of the fencing (particularly in winter when leaves off trees and hedges may allow weak areas and gaps to appear). Notice how in winter, when gateways become muddy and areas where horses are fed on the ground become poached, the quality of what the horses have to eat is reduced and the grazing limited. These areas may need some reseeding in the spring.

- Be aware that in the spring, as the ground dries and the sun promotes new growth, poisonous plants may develop; vigilant checking of the fields on a regular basis is needed.

- Get into the habit of observing horse paddocks and fields. Assess their good and bad points. Consider what features you would keep and what you would have to change if you chose to rent that field.

- Be aware of the variation in types of grassland according to the area in which you live. In a lowland area, where drainage may be less efficient, you may see many more reed-like grasses, which may not be of such good quality compared to a well-drained field in a fertile part of the country. Similarly, a field in a moorland or mountainous part of the country (parts of Wales or Scotland) may have sparse soil with poor grass.

- Consider fencing that is 'ideal' in terms of security and safety for the horses (e.g. post and rail) against what might be more affordable and provide greater protection from weather (an existing thick hedge).

- Similarly, be able to weigh up the pros and cons of different water supplies, and take into account what might be available (e.g. water trough or an existing stream).

- Be observant and practise running through the points in your mind as if you had been asked to give an opinion on the strengths and weaknesses of what you see. This is what you will need to be able to do with the assessor, so you must know your subjects thoroughly.

UNIT 4

Lunge a Horse Under Supervision

4 Credits

Lungeing

The candidate will be able to:

Lunge a horse

Work safely

The candidate will know:

How to lunge horses

The current health and safety legislation

In the lungeing section for Stage 2 you are now expected to fit the cavesson and side-reins and ensure that the rest of the tack is safe immediately before lungeing.

It is important to secure the stirrups. The best way to do this is as per the illustration opposite.

- Check that the side-reins are approximately the correct length by holding one end at the bit ring and the other at the middle of the saddle and then attach them either side. Put the loop end of the side-reins under the first and second girth straps and then undo the third girth strap, take it through the loop of the side-rein and re-attach to the girth. To be approximately the correct length, the side-rein should reach to the bit ring, be taut but not pull the horse's head behind the vertical. Do not attach the side-rein to the bit when tacking up – an approximation is fine. Clip the side-rein onto the D-ring on the other side of the withers, i.e. clip the nearside side-rein to the off -side and vice versa.

If you have somebody holding the horse for you, do talk to them and be polite. Take the opportunity to ask them the horse's name.

- Fit the cavesson as you would a bridle, i.e. take the leather out of the keepers and hold it against the horse's head for an approximation of fit.

- Fit the cavesson so that the noseband does not rub the protruding cheek bone, but not so low that it pinches the horse's skin between the noseband and the bit. For horses with a short face this can be difficult.

- The straps of the cavesson fit over or under the cheekpieces of the bridle depending on where they meet. Often the top strap of the cavesson (equivalent to the throatlash) will fit under the cheekpieces, and frequently the noseband of the cavesson will fit similarly between the cheekpieces and the horse's skin.

- The straps must be done up tightly enough so that the cavesson will not slide round the horse's head and into his eye as he is being lunged.

- Make sure you twist up the reins and put one of them through the throatlash.

Stirrups secured for lungeing so they will not slip down during exercise.

Correctly fitted side-reins. If there are three girth straps the side-rein should be under the first two straps.

145

- Remember it may be better to take your gloves off and put them in your pocket before you fit this equipment. If you do not have a pocket perhaps you could politely ask the person who is holding the horse if they would hold them for you.

- If the horse is not wearing boots all round you should ask your assessor if this horse is safe to be lunged without them on.

Method of lungeing

- When lungeing it is important that you position yourself and the horse correctly. You should think of a triangle – you are the apex, the horse is the base, and the lunge line and whip are the sides.

Good positioning of lunger in relation to the horse: handler in centre of circle; horse 'held' in a triangle between the lunge rein and the handler's whip and voice.

- You should stand approximately opposite the horse's girth area. If you stand too far in front of this you may stop the horse going forward, and if you are too far behind him you will continually be pulling him round rather than working for a light contact.

- Before you start lungeing always check your equipment. Make sure the girth and cavesson are tight and that the stirrups are secure. Ensure the side-reins are clipped to the D-rings on the saddle.

- The horse should wear boots all round (if, in the exam, he isn't, check with somebody who knows the horse that this is acceptable).

- Make sure your lunge line is not twisted. If you need to sort out the line it is acceptable to put it on the floor. To do this, make sure you are between the horse and the lunge line, and that there is no possibility of him or you treading on it. Do not attempt this with a lively horse or one you are unsure of. Be quick and efficient in collecting up the line into the format you use for lungeing. Some people lay the lunge line across their hand; others use loops. Both methods are acceptable as long as they are practised in a safe and efficient way. While doing this the whip should be held under your armpit, with the lash facing downwards behind you, away from the horse.

- The easiest way to start the lungeing process is to send the horse away from you using a firm 'Walk on' with your voice and pointing the whip towards the horse's hindquarters. Make sure that, as the horse walks away from you, you are not in a position where you can be kicked, or where the horse can pull away from you and carry straight on without going onto a circle.

- Your voice and body language are your main forms of command. Make sure you use a bright voice for upward transitions, and a more soothing one for downward transitions. With regard to your body language, you are in charge and the horse must realise this. Negative body language will imply lack of confidence to the horse (and the assessor). If you are too aggressive you will upset the horse. Consequently he may not settle and work well for you.

- To make a change of rein easy for you and the horse, try to stop the horse on the open side of the circle, away from the walls. Then once you have 'reeled in' the line as described below, stroke the horse on the neck, walk to the other side of him making sure you move the buckle of the line across to the other side of his nose and

Safe management of lunge equipment. Reins held in one hand or both, with elbows bent and thumbs on top (as when riding). Whip held in conjunction with the rein or alone.

then send him away from you. To change the rein like this ensures you do not have to 'drag' the horse across the circle, especially if you have side-reins on.

- The most common issue that people have with the lunge line is to keep it from becoming twisted when changing the rein. There are different methods of doing this but the easiest way is to ensure you change the line hand before you start collecting the line in. For instance, if you are on the right rein, change the line into the left hand, put the lunge whip up into your armpit with the lash on the ground behind you. Then, as you start to walk towards the horse, take the line through your right hand and put the loop into your left hand. Do not take your right hand off the line until you reach the horse's head and have looped the line into your left hand.

- It is advisable to lunge a horse on both reins before you consider putting on the side-reins. Never attach side-reins until the horse is going forwards, and only attach them if you feel it will be beneficial. Side-reins should be comfortable for the horse. There should be a light contact with the bit, to encourage him to work in a round frame, but they should not be so tight that they pull the head behind the vertical. Side-reins help with control and can improve the quality of the horse's work on the lunge. If you change the rein as discussed above you do not need to undo the side-reins. Always unclip the side-reins as soon as you have finished lungeing to allow the horse to stretch. Some people lunge the horse for a few minutes at the end of a session without the side-reins but there may not be time for this in a Stage 2 exam.

- Make sure that, when you want the horse to stop, you go out to meet him; you do not pull him into you, making the circle smaller and smaller. The horse should stop on the line of the circle and you then walk out to him.

- The whip is an essential part of the equipment when lungeing. It should never be used like a circus whip held high in the air and should be pointing towards the horse's point of hock. If you need to use it, a flick of your wrist in a sideways motion will ensure the lash moves to encourage the horse forward. If you actually need to make contact with the horse, then try and aim for the point of hock area or a little higher. Do not back off making contact with the whip if it is necessary, but always use it with discretion. When changing the rein, put the whip behind you and up into your armpit before reeling in the line. As long as you are careful with the lash and ensure neither you nor the horse can stand on it, then it is not necessary to pick it up when changing the rein. When bringing the whip round to move the horse forward after changing the rein, make sure you do this in a smooth movement that will not upset the horse.

Reasons for lungeing

- To start to train a young horse, making him obedient to the voice and learning to accept the tack.

- To work a horse that is unable to be ridden because, for some reason, he cannot wear a saddle (e.g. girth gall).

- To help build up muscle tone.

- To help improve suppleness.

- The rider cannot ride.

- To get rid of excess energy, e.g. at a competition.

- To help improve a rider's position.

- To start a horse over poles/fences.

- For variety within a training programme.

- To save time. Half an hour's correct lunge work is equivalent to at least one hour's ridden work.

What the assessor is looking for

- You will be required to lunge an established trained horse, one that should be obedient to your basic skills of control on the lunge in walk and trot on both reins.

- If you choose to canter the horse, that is up to you, but it is not expected at this stage. You should be asked to 'exercise' the horse. Be prepared to make the horse go forward adequately. Some well-trained, sensible lunge horses can verge on being lazy and may endeavour not to work very hard! If necessary, vary your voice to motivate the horse, and, if you have to, use the whip in an encouraging way (avoid letting it 'crack' in case this disturbs other horses in the school). If really necessary, then give the horse a sharp reminder with the end of the lash on his hock/buttock region to remind him to go forward.

- You should show approximately equal work on both reins with frequent transitions in and out of walk and trot (and canter if you feel confident and it helps to make the horse more forward).

- Your handling of the equipment should show a clear system of basic competence. Make sure that throughout the lungeing session you handle the rein and whip in such a way that it does not inconvenience either you or the horse, that it assists you in carrying out the lunge work competently, and is consistent – for example, make sure the rein is not twisted, and that you have control of the whip, particularly through the changes of rein.

- Your body language is extremely important, not just for the message you are sending to the assessor, but also for the message you are sending to the horse.

The assessor would like to see that you have an empathy with the horse and can determine whether he needs to be 'chased' a little or whether he is more sensitive and needs calming.

- Many horses used for lungeing at Stage 2 level are sensible, quiet types. It is essential that you encourage the horse to go forward. Many of these horses know exactly how long the lunge whip is and it may be necessary for you to walk a circle with the horse to get him going forward and to be able to use the lunge whip. If you have to walk, make sure it is on a circle and that you are dictating the shape and size, and not the horse. At frequent intervals try standing still and see if the horse will go forward without you having to move with him. Always make sure you are not walking/standing in front of the horse's eye line and thus stopping him psychologically from going forward. Do not be afraid to use the whip if necessary. Be tactful and accurate – do not use it like a circus whip.

- At Stage Two level it is not compulsory to use side-reins.

- After you have lunged the horse you will be asked some questions about lungeing. You may be asked to give some reasons for lungeing.

- You may be asked where you would lunge if there was not a surface to work on. The ideal place for this would be in the corner of a flat field where you would automatically have two sides enclosed to help. You could enclose the other two sides with barrels and poles if you felt it necessary. The going must be as good as possible. Old turf is fine, but if the ground is slippery, very muddy or stony the horse could lose his balance and injure himself. You should try very hard to avoid lungeing a horse in the middle of a big field – you may have control issues!

- You may be asked about the horse's basic way of going. When you are lungeing him make sure you are aware of the quality of his rhythm in the gaits you are asking him to work in. Is the rhythm consistent or does it vary all the time? How well balanced is he? If he has poor balance round a circle then the rhythm will be variable as he struggles to keep his balance. Does he look as if he is pulling himself around with his front legs, or is he pushing from behind and tracking up or over-tracking?

- A discussion may be held about when to use and when not to use side-reins. Remember you do not have to use side-reins at Stage 2 and, if the horse is not going forwards when you are lungeing him then do not use them. The side-reins should be pre-adjusted (at Stage 2 level) to the correct length, but always check as there may have been a last-minute issue that means they are not correct.

How to become competent

- Learning to fit a lungeing cavesson correctly needs some guidance. Lunge cavessons are specialist pieces of equipment and must fit snugly around the nose so that the attachment of the rein on the nose is comfortable. It is usually safer to apply the lunge cavesson immediately before the horse is taken from his stable. An unattended horse left tied up while wearing a lunge cavesson could become entangled or injured by the equipment.

- You must practise! Lungeing is not something you can learn to do competently unless you practise as much as possible.

- Your training should give you the basic system by which you:

  1. Fold the rein in your hand and manage it without twists.

  2. Manage the whip – as you lead the horse out to work, as you lunge, as you change the rein and as you finish, to lead in.

  3. Change the rein.

  4. Attach the side-reins.

  5. Undo the side-reins at the end of the exercise session.

  6. Understand the reason behind all the above procedures.

- To develop the competence in managing the very long rein, it can help to attach it to a fence, gate or similar fixed object and just get used to letting it out and taking it back up again, until you are completely at ease with the process. It is much more difficult when there is a horse at the end of the rein, so learn to manage the rein competently first.

- Similarly practise managing the whip, passing it from one hand to the other behind your back so that it does not interfere with the horse. If you manage the lash competently it is not necessary to pick it up every time you change the rein; it should be picked up at the start and end of a session when you are leading the horse in and out to the exercise area.

- Practise 'using' the whip in an active manner. It must be part of a co-ordinated procedure in which your voice, body stance and language, along with active movement of the whip as required, maintain the horse's respect for you and therefore your control over him.

- Learn to inject versatility into your voice. The horse will have little respect or obedience for a voice that is a whisper, or one that is very monotonous in tone.

- It is probably wise and good practice to have cantered a horse on the lunge. Although it is highly unlikely that you would be asked to canter a horse in a Stage 2 exam, if you have done it before, then you will be far more confident and competent. And if, in a worst-case scenario, the horse were to canter away on the lunge, or you were asked to include canter in your exercise, or you felt that a canter would help you to get the horse going more forward, you would then be better able to deal with these eventualities.

- Watch other people lungeing horses. It can help you immeasurably when you see people more capable than yourself dealing with the same sort of problems as you (for example, the rein going slack and brushing the floor; dropping the whip; or the rein becoming twisted).

- Remember: it is the overall competence that passes or fails you in the task, not the fact that, say, the rein briefly touched the floor or the whip slipped out of your hand!

- Experiment with different methods of holding the rein. Find the one which suits you best and which you can manage most successfully and efficiently.

- Make sure that you have understood the use of side-reins and how they are attached for lungeing.

- Understand that the horse must be forward before side-reins are attached, and that they must then be even in length. For this level of exam, the side-reins should already be fitted to suit the horse you will lunge. Your only decision is when to attach them, or whether or not to use them at all.

- If the horse is going forward easily for you, then attach the side-reins. These will help to keep the horse straight and give him a connection to work into from his activity. If the horse is 'creeping' around, and not actively forward, then the side-reins will probably not help and may actually further inhibit him from going more forward.

- Practise handling the side-reins so that you can attach them efficiently. You should not appear to fiddle with them for a long time. Once you start to use them, it should not be necessary to undo the side-reins to change the rein; only undo them to finish and lead the horse. When you undo the side-reins, secure them safely by clipping them back to the D-ring on the saddle on either side of the pommel.

- You can never practise lungeing enough.

STAGE 2

EQL Level 2 Diploma in BHS Riding Horses

IMPORTANT: Candidates are advised to check that they are working from the latest examination syllabus, as examination content and procedure are liable to alteration. Contact the BHS Examinations Office for up-to-date information regarding the syllabus.

Syllabus

Candidates are required to demonstrate their ability to ride a quiet, experienced horse or pony in an enclosed space without assistance. They must be competent and confident riding a strange horse on grass and over a show jumping course of up to 2ft 6in (76 cm). Their balance and security should indicate the correct foundation for future progress.

Candidates who are considered to be below the standard may be asked to retire.

FLAT
Ride Horses on the Flat in an Enclosed Area
21 credits/158 guided learning hours

Unit purpose and aims
The learner will be able to ride schooled horses independently and working as a ride in an enclosed environment. They must be confident and competent riding horses with and without stirrups in all three paces, and with the reins in one hand. Their position must be established, showing balance and security and a degree of 'feel'. They will be able to build up a rapport and work in harmony with various types of horse and show an understanding of the basic principles of riding from leg to hand. They will show an ability to assist the horse in keeping its balance during a range of school movements. The learners' independent, well balanced and secure seat should be established at this level. This will enable the learner to progress their confidence and competence in being able to further positively influence the horse's way of going.

Learner Outcomes		Assessment Criteria	
The learner will		The learner can	
1.	Be able to ride horses with a secure, independent and balanced position in walk, trot and canter, with and without stirrups	1.1	Walk, trot and canter with stirrups with a secure, independent and balanced position showing an ability to ride forward from leg to hand
		1.2	Ride with balance in walk, trot and canter
		1.3	Ride with 'suppleness' through the hip, knee and ankle joints in walk, trot and canter
		1.4	Ride using the correct diagonals in trot
		1.5	Walk, trot and canter without stirrups with a secure, independent and balanced position showing an ability to ride from leg to hand
2.	Be able to apply natural and artificial 'aids' for riding horses in an enclosed area	2.1	Prepare for and carry out school movements, maintaining the horse's rhythm and balance
		2.2	Use co-ordinated aids for riding transitions and school figures
		2.3	Maintain a suitable rein contact for the work undertaken
		2.4	Utilise natural and artificial aids as required.
		2.5	Use co-ordinated aids for riding with the reins in one hand
		2.6	Use co-ordinated aids to prepare for and ensure a correct canter lead
3.	Be able to ride horses in harmony and in conjunction with others using the area	3.1	Show respect for the horse and build up a rapport when riding
		3.2	Abide by the rules of the school when riding with others in closed and open order
4.	Know the principles of the horse's way of going	4.1	Describe the horse's behaviour and responses to the aids and surroundings whilst being ridden
		4.2	Describe the way of going of the ridden horse
		4.3	Describe the aids used on the ridden horse

JUMPING
Ride Horses over Fences in an Enclosed Area
21 credits/158 guided learning hours

Unit purpose and aims
The learner will be able to show a secure, independent balanced jumping position. They must be confident and competent jumping horses over a course of fences up to maximum of 2ft 6ins (76cm). Their position must be established, showing balance and security and a degree of 'feel'. They will be able to build up a rapport and work in harmony with various types of horse. They will show an ability to assist the horse in keeping its balance round a course of fences. The learners' independent and well balanced jumping position should be established at this level. This will enable the learner to develop their skills and ability to jump horses over more difficult fences and courses.

Learner Outcomes		Assessment Criteria	
The learner will		The learner can	
1.	Be able to walk a show jump course	1.1	Walk a route suitable for riding a show jump course
2.	Be able to ride in preparation for jumping including a grid of fences	2.1	Maintain a secure, independent and balanced position at trot and canter, with stirrups of a suitable length for jumping
		2.2	Ride safely according to the ground and weather conditions to maintain the horse's balance
		2.3	Jump through a grid of fences in 'harmony' with the horse
3.	Be able to jump horses over a course of fences up to maximum of 2ft 6ins (76cm)	3.1	Ride horses over a course of fences in a secure, independent and balanced jump position
		3.2	Use co-ordinated aids to ride horses over a course of fences
		3.3	Maintain a suitable rein contact at all times
		3.4	Show an effective control of pace
		3.5	Utilise natural and artificial aids as required
4.	Be able to ride and jump horses in harmony and in with an awareness of other riders	4.1	Show respect for the horse and build up a rapport when riding
		4.2	Jump horses with confidence
		4.3	Ride horses in harmony, to produce a fluently ridden course
		4.4	Ride safely with others
5.	Know the principles of the horse's way of going	5.1	Describe the horse's behaviour whilst being ridden
		5.2	Describe the way of going of the ridden horse
		5.3	Describe the aids used on the ridden horse

Ride Horses on the Flat in an Enclosed Area

21 Credits

The candidate should be able to:

Ride horses with a secure, independent and balanced position in walk, trot and canter with and without stirrups

What the assessor is looking for

- A basically correct riding position is the foundation for all your work and your future as an effective, competent rider. You will be expected to show this as a Stage 2 level rider.

- The rider must sit centrally in the saddle with even weight on both seat bones, with level stirrups and even weight on the balls of the feet, the heel a little deeper than the toe. The upper body should rise tall and supple above the seat, with an imaginary vertical line from the rider's ear, through the shoulder, hip and heel. Hands should be level above the withers, with another imaginary straight line running from the elbow, through the wrist, the rein and to the horse's mouth. Hands should be closed around the reins, with the thumbs uppermost and the wrist relaxed.

- A good basic riding position shows some suppleness and relaxation. This is

Correct basic riding position. Note straight line ear–shoulder–hip–heel; and also elbow–wrist–rein–horse's mouth.

achieved through the secure development of the position. You must show an ability to follow the movement of the horses you ride, maintaining elasticity and 'feel' for the horse's movement under you.

- You must show an independent seat, which at no time, or in any of the basic gaits, is reliant on the reins. This independence must be demonstrated on at least two different horses on the flat (and later on two horses jumping). You will be asked to ride school movements to include turns, circles and transitions. These must demonstrate your independence and balance with the horse.

How to become competent

- The only way to develop a deeper, more secure riding position is to ride as much as possible. Try to ride under instruction on a regular basis so that your instructor can help you to improve and work on your position. It is easy, otherwise, to slip into bad habits, which can easily become established as firm faults and are then difficult to correct.

- If you can be lunged regularly, this is an ideal way of being able to work on your position and 'feel' without having to concentrate on the control of the horse.

- Ride as many different horses as you can to give you experience and confidence in being able to ride any horse that might be offered to you.

- Work regularly without your stirrups so that you progressively develop a deeper, more secure and more supple position.

- Ride horses out and about, hacking and in any type of off-road country, where you can truly develop your skill and control in the 'big outdoors'.

- Ride in a group fairly often. Be careful that you do not spend too long riding in a school with no other riders present. This does not develop your independence in terms of finding space and becoming competent when several other riders are using the same space.

- Practise school movements at every opportunity. Make sure that your preparation for turns, circles and transitions is good. The way in which you prepare and execute movements says much about your awareness, feel and effect as a rider.

The candidate should be able to:

Apply natural and artificial 'aids' for riding horses in an enclosed area

What the assessor is looking for

- Throughout all your riding you must try to establish a rapport and a partnership with each horse you ride. This is not easy when you may be nervous, and when you ride the horse for only a brief period of about 20 minutes. Prioritise riding the horse forward into an active gait and then concentrate on maintaining as good a rhythm (regularity) as you can.

- Be prepared to use your legs effectively, and if the horse is lazy and unresponsive to your legs, then demonstrate your ability to use your whip with good timing to remind the horse that he must obey your leg.

- Having established a forward-going and rhythmical gait then use this to demonstrate that you can ride well prepared and accurate turns and circles. When riding school figures you must show that you are aware of the tempo (speed of the gait) and can sustain the rhythm and balance of the horse within the movements.

Riding a good-shaped circle, with the horse maintaining a consistent bend following the perimeter line of the circle.

Reins rather long, so contact is slack; rider's hands almost in her waist.

Reins too short. Rider showing tension in the arms and restricting the horse, who is tight and short in the neck.

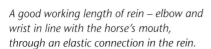

A good working length of rein – elbow and wrist in line with the horse's mouth, through an elastic connection in the rein.

- Rein contact comes from your ability to ride the horse forward effectively in balance and rhythm and then to be secure and independent enough in your position to be able to maintain a good contact with the horse's mouth.

- The 'connection' with the horse's mouth must come from riding forward from leg to hand.

- The reins must be short enough that you demonstrate a consistent connection, but the contact is always established from the activity of the horse's hind legs. You must be able to demonstrate an 'allowing hand', i.e. one which 'feels' the mouth but does not hang on to it or restrict the horse.

- You will be required to ride without your stirrups in walk, trot and canter. During this work you must show a depth and security of position that allows you to maintain an independent hand. Assessors are looking for you to be established enough to demonstrate a suppleness and ability to 'move' with the horse with no dependence on the reins to sustain balance.

- Be aware that being able to 'stay on' the horse in all three gaits will not prove your competence. Assessors are looking for established riders who are independent of their hands, and beginning to show a clear harmony and empathy with the horses they ride. The rider's security and balance allows an effective application of the aids and therefore harmonious influence on the horse.

Reins in one hand, the free hand relaxed by the rider's side and the position well maintained. The free hand should not carry the whip.

- The independence of your seat will be further proved when you are asked to ride with the reins in one hand. Take the reins in your outside hand, put your whip into your outside hand but leave it on the inside of the horse, so it crosses over the withers. Allow your inside hand to hang loosely down by your side. The relaxation in your fingers (of the free hand) shows your suppleness and co-ordination. When you change the rein, change the reins into the other hand also, so that the inside hand is free. (If, however, you are simply riding a figure-of-eight across long diagonals you probably won't have time to change hands.) You must be able to maintain balance and control of the horse while you have the reins in one hand.

- Correct and co-ordinated application of aids comes from a secure, independent position giving the ability to clearly apply leg and hand aids in a manner to which the horse can respond smoothly and obediently.

- You must have a clear understanding of what aids you are trying to apply for specific transitions or school movements, then show that you can apply them in a co-ordinated way.

- Co-ordinated aid application comes from good preparation. Preparation begins with the thought process: think in plenty of time ahead of when you require the movement or transition to happen. This will enable you to consider the aids you wish to apply, give you time to apply those aids in a smooth, clear way, and allow time for the horse to recognise the aids and respond to them. The end result should be smooth transitions from one gait to another and fluent delivery of figures and school movements.

- At Stage 2 you will be expected to make active, fluent transitions from trot to canter (and from canter back to trot). The horse will naturally establish the correct sequence of legs in canter for the direction in which he is going, unless he is unbalanced or disturbed by the rider. It is therefore important that you are aware of the correct balance of the horse to enable him to answer your aids with a correct strike-off.

- It is often easier for the horse to give you a correct strike-off in a corner, because here the natural direction of the curve should encourage the horse to take the correct leading leg. On an unfamiliar horse it is therefore advisable to ask for canter in a corner to help ensure that the strike-off is correct.

- Prepare for the transition to canter well before the corner; think ahead, and take a few strides of sitting trot before the corner. The aids would be:

    - apply your inside leg on the girth to produce and maintain energy;

    - place your outside leg behind the girth to ask the horse to strike-off into canter;

    - use your inside hand to create a little flexion in the direction in which you are going;

    - use your outside hand to regulate the flexion and also control the gait so that the speed of the trot does not increase as you ask for canter.

- You are likely to be asked to ride such figures as 20m, 15m and perhaps 10m circles, serpentines, loops, turns across the school or down the centre line, and inclines on the long or short diagonal to change the rein.

- Much of the work will be done in open order. Get into the habit of never going all the way round the outside of the school without doing something – a school figure, transition, or turn.

How to become competent

- To be really confident in your riding ability at this level, you should be riding as often as possible. Ideally this should be every day, but realistically it may be four or five times per week.

- Riding under instruction will progress your technical competence, because the input from your instructor should consolidate your knowledge of what you are trying to achieve with the horse. Training will also ensure that you do not develop bad faults or habits in your riding position and in your overall manner of preparing and executing movements.

- It is very important that you ride as many horses as possible, and that, whenever you can, you ride under your own initiative. This will help you to develop independence and self-sufficiency.

- It is easy to become dependent on your instructor and use him or her as a support to your riding competence. It is essential that you feel equally secure in your ability to produce good work whether you ride alone or under instruction. You will then feel confident in an exam situation when you may be nervous and you have no support from your instructor to keep you going.

- Ride in the school and hack out. Take part in whatever ridden activities you can, such as pleasure rides, clear-round jumping or Riding Club type competitions. Doing so will develop your all-round skills as a rider.

- If you have your own horse and are a regular competitor in any discipline then this will also prove extremely helpful. The more riding you have done independently, learning to 'feel' and find out about the horse from your own experience, the more this will consolidate and complement good training.

- Ride as often as you can without stirrups. Ideally you should spend a little time on this every time you ride. You will then feel entirely comfortable without your stirrups. If you have regularly worked through all three gaits on a variety of different horses, it should feel as familiar to you to ride without your stirrups as with them.

- Similarly, practise riding with the reins in one hand. We all need to work on our co-ordination to some degree and the more often you practise a skill, the more competent you become.

- Practise riding figures and changes of direction with the reins in one hand. Feel familiar doing this on more than one horse. Make sure that you can also manage your whip when your reins are in one hand. (Hold the whip under the thumb of your rein hand – but down the opposite side of the neck.) Do not carry the whip in your free hand.

- Learn to 'feel' the canter. In the early stages you may need to 'look' for the leading leg in canter, which is preferable to failing to recognise if you are on the incorrect lead and allowing the horse, and even encouraging him, to keep cantering in an unbalanced way.

- The more you prepare the horse and the more clearly you apply the correct aids, the more likely the horse is to respond obediently and give you the correct lead.

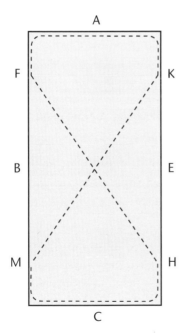

Changes of rein on the long diagonal.

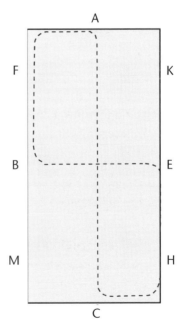

Changes of rein across the school and down centre line.

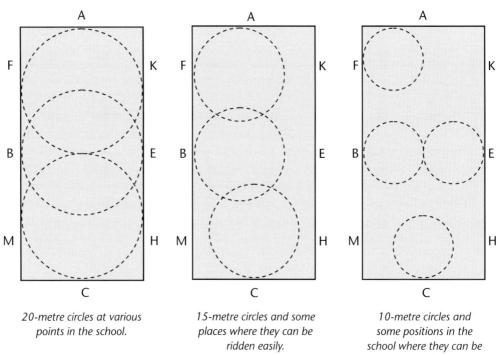

20-metre circles at various points in the school.

15-metre circles and some places where they can be ridden easily.

10-metre circles and some positions in the school where they can be used.

- Until you can 'feel' the correct leg, learn to glance down to check the leading leg without this affecting your whole position. Gradually learn to recognise the unbalanced feeling you get from the horse when he is on the incorrect lead.

- If the horse does strike-off on the 'wrong leg' this is not a major problem as long as you deal with it in a constructive way. Always bring the horse back to trot as soon as you recognise that the lead is incorrect. Rebalance the trot, and re-establish the rhythm and control of the trot. Then prepare again and in an appropriate corner ask for the canter again. If you do this, you will be given far more credit for taking control of the incorrect lead, than if you panic and try to chase the horse back into canter at any price, in which case the chances are he will offer the incorrect lead again because you may not have rebalanced and prepared him clearly enough. Go through the same remedial process again, if necessary.

- Riding good school figures and movements comes with practice. First you must understand the figure you are trying to ride and exactly where it should be positioned in the school. Sometimes it can help you to draw the various school movements on a piece of graph paper so that you can visualise the 'floor pattern'. Draw to scale a 20m by 40m rectangle (to represent a standard arena) and add the markers (arena letters) in the appropriate positions. Then outline the various figures in such a way that you can see exactly where they fit in the arena. Commit this to memory and it should help you when you next come to ride the figures on a horse.

- Make sure that you know the aids for basic transitions, figures and movements. If you are familiar with the aids then you should not be struggling to remember which leg goes where. If you are not sure, then the overall communication with the horse will be affected and this will be mirrored in your performance.

- Preparation is a key word. While you can rarely prepare too much, your preparation must remain subtle (especially the thought process) so that the horse does not start to anticipate and react before you ask him. It is very easy, however, not to make enough preparation, which will result in a loss of harmony or effect, or both.

- Some horses will give you a better 'feel' than others. As already mentioned, feel comes with practice and needs nurturing and developing. Each horse you ride will give you a slightly different feeling and therefore each new horse you ride should teach you something a little different.

The candidate should be able to:

Ride horses in harmony and in conjunction with others using the area

What the assessor is looking for

- You must try to ride with confidence and demonstrate your competence at this level. This will enable the horse to relax and work with you and then harmony will be the result.

- Try to forget that you are riding in an exam in front of people assessing your competence. Imagine you are riding a new horse at home and you are keen to find out about him and are enjoying the challenge of learning something new about him. Work to a clear system with thought and preparation for all you do.

The horse will then respond to your consistency and the result should be a partnership.

- Fluent, unconstrained work will be reflected in forward, rhythmical gaits in walk, trot and canter. The work should look smooth, accurate and well prepared, with the horse moving easily from one movement to another through clearly recognisable figures and changes of rein.

- You must look as if your whole concentration is on achieving a partnership with the horse; you want to be seen as effective and relaxed in your quest for good, consistent work.

- Safe riding develops with knowledge and control. You must be aware of, and abide by, the rules for riding in enclosed areas with other riders.

Illustration of some of the rules for riding in company in an enclosed area.

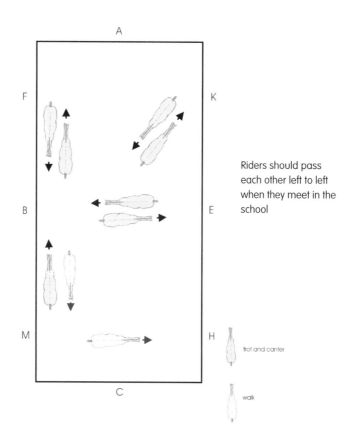

Riders should pass each other left to left when they meet in the school

Walk should be used on the inner track, giving priority to those trotting or cantering on the track

trot and canter

walk

- As a novice rider your instructor will take most, if not all, of the responsibility for your safety while on the horse. This responsibility is something that increasingly becomes yours as your ability as a rider develops.

- Awareness is essential for you to begin to recognise a potentially unsafe situation and to avoid putting yourself in such a position. (For example, riding too close to the horse in front puts you and/or your horse at risk of being kicked.)

- Control of your horse comes through preparation (including that all-important process: thinking ahead), with clear execution of aids to enable you to clearly influence the horse with good timing.

- Rules for enclosed riding areas include:

  - a procedure for entering and leaving the arena, especially when other riders are using the school;

  - walking on a good inside track;

  - passing other riders left hand to left hand;

  - giving way to others in a faster gait or more difficult movement;

  - being aware of riders who may be in difficulty and giving them space to regain control;

  - turning across the school to execute downward transitions.

How to become competent

- Become familiar with riding lots of different horses under instruction and independently. Learn to 'feel' the horse and 'read' the horse so that you understand why he might be responding (or not) to you.

- Develop confidence in your ability to be more effective with lazy horses and to be tactful and quiet on 'sharper' horses. Reward the horse with a pat on the neck (or a quiet word) when he responds to you in a positive way, particularly if you have had to use the whip to produce a reaction.

- Be aware of what is forward, rhythmical and harmonious and what is tense, anxious and hurried or lazy and 'behind the leg'.

- The chances are that the establishment where you ride and/or train has a specific set of rules by which it expects its riders (you) to abide. Make sure that you have studied these and that you apply them every time you ride in the school in company.

- Be prepared to adhere specifically to the guidelines which are there to ensure your safety and that of the horse you are riding and other riders around you.

- If in doubt as to your control when riding in company, always reduce your pace first. This gives you a better chance to maintain or regain control of your horse.

- Always ride purposefully and forward. If you ride cautiously in company, sometimes your horse will become nervous and be inclined to spook away from other horses approaching him, only because you are not riding him confidently and making him feel secure.

- When riding in company in an enclosed area, learn to look ahead and gauge when to circle away into space if you are becoming too close to another rider.

- The more you practise riding independently in a school in open order with other riders, the more capable and safe you will be.

- You should have a basic understanding of the scales of training and be able to apply the first three scales to the horses you ride. The scales of training can be translated in different ways but most people agree they are:

  1. Rhythm/regularity

  2. Suppleness/relaxation

  3. Contact/connection

  4. Impulsion

  5. Straightness

  6. Collection

- You should try to recognise if the horse you are riding is going forward in good rhythm, keeping his balance when performing school figures and transitions and is accepting a light contact. This relates to the first three scales of training and is sufficient for Stage 2 Level.

JUMPING

Ride Horses over Fences in an Enclosed Area

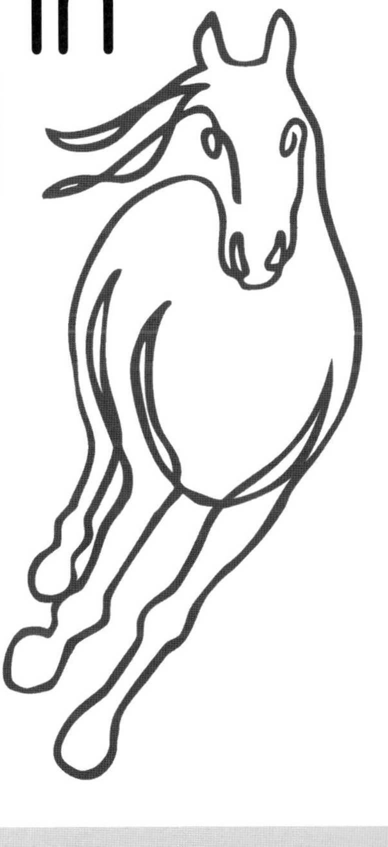

21 Credits

The candidate should be able to

Walk a show jump course

You should arrive at the exam early enough to allow yourself plenty of time to walk the show jump course without being rushed. It is advisable to bring a pair of wellingtons or other boots that you can wear when walking the course so that you can keep your riding boots clean.

There should be a diagram of the courses available for you to look at. Study it carefully and then start to walk the course. The fences will be clearly numbered. When walking any show jump course always walk the lines you are going to take. Do not cut the corners. The line you walk should make sure you approach the middle of each fence at right angles. Try to walk a smooth line away from the fence that ensures you use as much space as is available. It is not a jump-off against the clock so there is no need to try to cut corners.

It is essential that you make the effort to really concentrate when walking the course. If you know where you are going you will be able to look from fence to fence when riding. The horse will then be able to follow you and this will help him to keep his balance and rhythm.

The candidate should be able to

Ride in preparation for jumping including a grid of fences

What the assessor is looking for

Rider position demonstrated through the phases of the horse's jump from approach, take off, in flight in the air, to landing and departure.

- You must demonstrate control of the horse and balance in your position. It is likely that taking your stirrups up one or two holes will enable you to demonstrate this balance and control when riding outside on undulating ground and in due course for jumping a course of fences.

- Your balanced position in harmony with the horse is tested throughout.

- You must show co-ordination in your leg and rein aids but also show effectiveness with your legs to sustain a fluent, forward pace for your riding outside and your course when jumping.

- Rein aids must demonstrate balance and feel.

- You must show balance and harmony with the horse in an open space, a large grass field or similar unmarked area, showing awareness of other riders.

- The position adopted would be appropriate to the gait in which you choose to ride.

- You may feel the need to ride with your stirrups one or two holes shorter than you would in the school, when riding outside.

Maintaining a balanced position with the horse going up and down hill.

- You may choose to adopt a slightly lighter seat or jumping position; however, an upright position is also perfectly acceptable.

- The emphasis must be on the rider's balance and feel of moving with the horse.

- The rider must show judgement and choose the appropriate gait for riding over undulating ground, taking into account the ground conditions. You may be asked questions by the assessor about riding in varying weather conditions outside and over undulating ground, if this has not been demonstrated in the riding outside.

How to become competent

- There is no substitute for practice. Ride as many different horses as possible. Develop balance and co-ordination in all gaits. Include some faster canter work if you can, so that you learn to balance with a shorter stirrup and broader base of position, which gives you the security to work at faster gaits and to jump.

- You must jump as often as you can so that it is familiar to you and not something you do just to prepare for your exam.

- If you can do some pleasure rides, cross-country schooling, or any form of jumping competition, this will develop your competence, familiarity with riding out of the comfort zone of the indoor/outdoor school, and therefore your confidence.

Jumping position with slight variations on upper body angle, which may be used on different horses or in show jumping or cross-country riding.

- Make sure that your instructor supervises your work and checks your position from time to time. This will ensure that you are working in the best balance possible and that you have made best use of the appropriate stirrup length, which as a rough guide should be one to four holes shorter than your normal 'flat-work' riding length.

- The more you can hack out on different horses, experience riding along bridleways, common land, moorland, beach or forest land, the better. This will develop your self-sufficiency and the initiative to 'manage' any circumstances which arise.

- Riding out and about will teach you to 'feel' the horse's balance under you and to learn to adapt your position to enable him to carry you with maximum comfort and minimum effort and inconvenience.

- Riding other than in a 'controlled' marked-out arena under the direction of your instructor, will enable you to 'experiment' with your position and help you to learn to feel when the horse manages you most easily.

- In the school continue to practise plenty of work without stirrups to further deepen your position.

- Practise walk, trot and canter without stirrups, and also without stirrups in jumping position.

- Practise changing your position from upright to jumping position and back again in all three gaits.

- Ride outside at different times of the year and learn to feel how a horse balances himself when the ground is deep, slippery or hard.

- Learn to recognise the difference in how the horse moves from one gait to another when he is finding it more difficult to maintain balance on awkward ground.

- Watch other riders riding in difficult conditions and see how they adjust their gait or their position to help the horse.

The candidate should be able to:

Jump horses over a course of fences up to maximum 2ft 6in (76cm)

What the assessor is looking for

- The key here is 'security and balance'. Very simply if you are secure through a supple, well-established position on the flat, which then enables you to ride in a good balance over undulating ground and follow the horse fluently when jumping, then you will be demonstrating competence at Stage 2 level.

- It is important that you can show an understanding of the effective control of pace. The horse should be active and obediently forward, without being either lazy or too 'sharp' and then running against the hand and compromising the rider's control and authority.

Rider in balance over a fence.

- It is important that you demonstrate an attempt to achieve harmony with the horse. If he is lazy then you must show a clear pathway to be able to influence him with authority so that he responds. This may involve the well-timed use of the whip. It is just as important that, after using the whip, and, it is hoped, achieving a response, you praise the horse (with a pat on the neck or words of encouragement). He then understands the aid you have given and he has been reassured by the praise, being aware that the use of the whip is a reminder to obey the leg aid, not a punishment.

- Your jumping will be assessed on two horses. On the first horse you will work up to a small grid of two small fences, which will be built up gradually. You may start with a cross-pole (with or without a placing pole) and you will probably be asked to approach in trot.

- Aim to have enough energy in the trot approach so that the horse jumps the fence actively and lands in canter. He should have enough impulsion to maintain the canter fluently as he moves away from the fence.

- As two fences are then built up, it is likely that there will be one or two non-jumping strides between the first and second. The two fences are regarded as a small 'grid' exercise.

- You should show an ability to create an active approach but not allow the horse to hurry or take control. Keep the horse straight through the centre of the fences and maintain a good feel and balance in the approach, over the fence and in the departure.

- This work will then follow into the riding of a small course of about 2ft 6in (76cm). Your ability to keep a fluent pace around the jumps will be assessed. You must show that you can ride straight lines of approach and departure, keeping the horse energetic around corners, in readiness for presentation to the next fence.

- The fluency and smoothness of the course will be affected if the horse is unbalanced, particularly around corners. This may be evident by a wrong leading leg in canter. An incorrect lead is not a point of failure in itself. If the horse is on the wrong leg, particularly if this happens repeatedly, and you show no apparent awareness of the bad effect it is having on him, then this would be considered a weakness at this level.

You may be asked how you felt one of the horses you rode behaved during the jumping section. You need to talk about such things as the following. How obedient was he to your aids? Was he responsive or did he appear to ignore you? How consistent were the rhythm and balance? Was he able to keep his balance? Did he try to rush the fences? How forward-thinking and amenable was he? Was he worried about jumping any of the fences? Was he nappy when he went past the other horses?

How to become competent

- By working to improve your basic riding position with frequent work without stirrups, ongoing training from your instructor and as much riding as possible on a variety of horses, your depth and security of seat will gradually get better and better. In conjunction with this, taking your stirrups up and practising the jumping position in all three gaits will develop your feel and balance in the light seat position.

- An excellent exercise to improve this overall balance and competence is to work in trot and canter in a 'standing up' position. This will ensure that you both 'feel' your balance and develop it, because you can only do this exercise well if you have achieved that balance and flexibility over your lower leg.

- Ride without stirrups, both in your ordinary flatwork and also in pole work (during which you can practise jumping position without stirrups). Gradually work without stirrups over small fences, and eventually aim to feel more secure and independent without your stirrups than you do with them.

- Riding a horse without a saddle (bareback) also improves your feel and balance. You cannot 'grip' to stay on, as this will inevitably cause you to slip and slide around. Riding bareback encourages you to relax and move with the movement of the horse, because it is easy to feel the horse's movement directly underneath you. It is wise, though, to ride bareback in an enclosed, controlled situation on a horse you know well.

- You must try to ride and jump several different horses, inside and out. Learn to 'feel' how the horse is moving underneath you. While you may need to 'look' for the leading leg to start with, in time, and with practice, you should develop an increasing awareness of whether the lead is correct or not.

- Try to 'feel' the influence of such things as different 'going' underfoot, gradients,

Riding bareback, on a horse you know well, will improve your balance, feel and security.

and foothold. Particularly in the 'field,' recognise how the horse changes his way of going to be able to balance himself (and you on top) up and down hills, in heavy going such as deep mud or plough, on hard ground or a slippery surface. Notice if, in canter, the horse changes leg or becomes disunited, or even loses the canter, because of the ground conditions.

- Once you begin to notice the changes then you can feel how your balance affects the horse, and begin to ride with an increasing awareness of maintaining the horse's balance and impulsion.

- Practise your jumping whenever possible. Try to make sure that you ride horses that are genuine and honest to a fence. Horses that maintain a steady and consistent rhythm to the fence are ideal because you should not be disturbed and seeking to regain your balance within the last few strides in front of the fence.

- If you do not feel confident about jumping horses you do not know to a height of 2ft 6in (76cm) then you should re-consider entering for the jumping unit of the Stage 2 exam.

- You need to practise talking about the horses you ride. Ask your instructor to ask you questions about how the horses you have ridden have jumped.

- Try to get into the habit of saying something positive about the horse first and, without being too critical, try to be truthful.

- Try to get your thoughts together before you start speaking. This will help you to get your breath back after the course and you will not sound so flustered or uncertain.

STAGE 2

Questions and Answers

On the following pages are some of the suggested questions/tasks from the Stage 2 syllabus. Each question is listed with a concise answer offering acceptable knowledge. In every case you should try to enhance your answer to give a more comprehensive indication of your depth of knowledge. A more expansive answer requires that you study each subject a little more deeply, which will enable you to speak with greater confidence in giving your answers.

Shoeing

Q. What procedure does the farrier follow when shoeing a horse?
A. Tie up the horse.

Remove the shoes using buffer, hammer and pincers.

Trim the foot for excess horn growth.

Prepare the shoe and the foot for the new shoe.

If hot shoeing, burns the shoe on the hoof to ensure size and fit.

Nail on the shoe starting at the toe and working on alternate sides to the heels.

Hammer down the clenches and rasp the finished foot lightly, to produce a smooth end-result.

Q. What problems arise from leaving shoes on too long?
A. The foot will overgrow the shoe and there might be injury or lameness.

The shoe may embed into the foot and cause corns or other pressure points, and discomfort.

The shoe may loosen and move on the foot, or be pulled off.

The horse's foot balance is affected by shoes that are not maintained and this could cause lameness.

Clipping and Trimming

Q. Why do we need to clip horses?
A. Horses are clipped usually in the winter when they develop a thick, protective winter coat. When they are worked they sweat profusely under their thick coat and then may get cold when drying off. Clipping enables the horse to work comfortably with less sweating.

Q. When and how often might they need clipping?
A. Horses usually need clipping any time from mid September onwards, depending on how quickly their winter coat comes through. They usually need clipping every three weeks until the end of the year and then less frequently in the early part of the New Year when the winter coat has stopped growing.

Q. What types of clip are there and when might they be used?
A. The following clips might be used: trace clip, chaser clip, blanket clip, hunter clip, full clip, 'neck and belly'. Different clips are used according to what type of work the horse might be doing. The harder the work, the more the horse is clipped.

Q. What types of clipping machines are available?

A. There are large commercial-type machines for clipping many horses. There are smaller electric clippers with blades of different grades coarseness/ fineness.There are small battery-operated clippers which are quieter for nervous horses or for use around the head.

Q. What checks would you make before use?

A. Check the machine is well maintained, oiled and has been serviced. Make sure that you have a sharp pair of blades.

Make sure the flex is complete and undamaged.

Make sure you are using a circuit-breaker for the electrical source.

Make sure that you have a safe stable in which to tie the horse.

Make sure you have assistance available in case you need help.

Q. What care do they need before, during and after use?

A. Machines should be annually checked and serviced. Blades should be resharpened. During clipping regularly turn off the machine so that it does not get too hot and is allowed to cool down. Remove the blades and wipe them and oil them before replacing them. After use the blades should be cleaned, oiled and stored separately while the machine is cleaned of all hair and then oiled and put away.

Q. Why should a circuit-breaker be used and where should it be positioned?

A. A circuit-breaker protects the user of an electrical appliance from receiving a shock in the event of a problem in the power source. It should be fitted in the plug socket and then the clippers' plug is inserted into it.

Anatomy and Physiology

Q. Discuss the health, condition and fitness of a horse.

A. Be able to talk about a horse in front of you, making observations about his state of health/well-being (shiny flexible coat/clear bright eyes/alert/at ease/carrying an appropriate amount of weight for the work he is doing).

Be able to discuss the fitness of the horse i.e. his ability to carry out work. (muscle tone/weight/'clean' legs/'cool' legs.)

Q. How does a horse gather food into his mouth?

A. He 'picks' with his lips, tears with his front (incisor) teeth and then pushes the food into the mouth and towards his back (molar) teeth with his tongue.

185

Q. **What are the functions of the following: the lips, the incisor teeth, the tongue, the molar teeth?**

A. The lips – pick the food (grass).

The incisor teeth – tear or cut the food.

The tongue – pushes food to the back of the mouth.

The molar teeth – grind or pulverise the food.

Q. **What is the alimentary canal?**

A. The digestive tract of the horse from his mouth to his anus.

Q. **Where is the gullet?**

A. In the horse's neck joining his mouth to his stomach.

Q. **What is its other name?**

A. The oesophagus.

Q. **Can you point it out on the horse?**

A. Underside of the neck.

Q. **When the horse is eating can you feel and observe when the food passes down the gullet?**

A. Yes.

Q. **What size is the horse's stomach?**

A. Approximately the size of a rugby football with a capacity of 2-4 gallons (9–18 litres).

Q. **What influence does the size of the stomach have on the way the horse is fed and worked?**

A. Because of a relatively small stomach in comparison to the horse's size, he must be fed small amounts of food at a time, so that the volume capacity of the stomach is not overloaded. Frequent small amounts of food will mimic the way the horse would browse naturally in the wild and therefore be most compatible with keeping him healthy.

Q. **How long is it before food entering the horse leaves the stomach?**

A. This process begins after approximately one hour, but it is ongoing and for the stomach to completely empty its contents will take up to 24 hours. However the stomach should have an ongoing supply of food coming into it regularly.

Q. What are the parts of the alimentary canal after the stomach?

A. The stomach is followed by the small intestine which is made up of three parts: the duodenum, the jejunum and the ileum. The small intestine opens into the large intestine which is made up of the caecum, the large colon, the small colon and then the rectum and the anus.

Q. Why is it important that any change of diet should be introduced slowly?

A. The digestive process in the large intestine is assisted by the presence of 'gut flora' – microbes which help to break down the food into its component parts. If the diet is suddenly changed some of these 'good' microbes may not be able to process the 'new' food and some may not be present that are necessary for the digestion of the 'new' food. Gradual change of diet allows the appropriate microbes to be maintained or evolved to deal with whatever food enters the digestive tract.

Q. Horses cannot be sick (vomit). Is this a disadvantage?

A. Yes, because they are unable to get rid of anything which might be alien or damaging to them other than passing it right through the system, which inevitably takes time and may render them fairly ill in the meantime.

Q. Designate the following parts of the horse's skeleton on the horse in front of you:

1. **The mandible or jawbone, the occipital bone, the atlas, the axis.**
2. **The cervical vertebrae and their number.** (7 cervical vertebrae: the atlas, the axis and five more. Make sure when showing where these are that you follow the correct line – not the crest.)
3. **The thoracic vertebrae and their number.** (18 thoracic vertebrae.)
4. **The lumbar vertebrae and their number.** (6 lumbar vertebrae.)
5. **The sacral vertebrae and their number.** (5 sacral vertebrae.)
6. **The coccygeal vertebrae and their number.** (15 to 21 coccygeal vertebrae.)
7. **What are the spinal processes?** These are bony vertical and transverse extensions of the vertebrae which aid muscle attachment.
8. **Where is the sternum?** In the chest, between the ribs. **What else may it be called?** Also called the 'breast bone'.
9. **Where are the ribs? How many are there? Why are some described as true ribs and some as false ribs?** The ribs are in the chest cavity; there are 18 pairs and those that are attached to the spine and the sternum are called 'true' ribs

(8 pairs); those attached to the spine and only cartilage at the other end are known as 'false or floating' ribs (10 pairs).

10. **Name and designate the bones of the forehand.** Head, neck, shoulders and forelegs, as far as the withers; skull, cervical vertebrae, shoulder, humerus, radius, carpus, cannon bone, splint bones (2), sesamoids (2), long and short pastern, navicular and pedal bones.

11. **Name and designate the bones which form the hind leg of the horse.** Pelvis, femur, fibula, tibia, patella, stifle joint, hock joint, os calcis, then from the cannon bone down the limb is the same as the foreleg.

12. **Where is the equivalent on the horse of the human joints of the knee, wrist, ankle and elbow?** Knee = horse's patella/stifle; wrist = horse's knee; ankle = horse's hock; elbow = horse's elbow.

Q. Describe the structure of the horse's foot and designate the external parts.

A. The horse's foot is like an enclosed box with all the internal structures held within the horny outer hoof.

Be able to point to: the wall, coronary band, bulbs of the heels, sole, frog, bars, white line, pastern, and fetlock joint.

Q. What is the function of the frog?

A. It is the 'shock-absorber' for the foot, adding 'grip' when it contacts the ground, and it assists in pushing the blood back up the leg to maintain circulation.

Q. Why is the white line so important?

A. It shows externally the join between the insensitive parts and the sensitive parts of the foot.

Q. What daily care is needed to keep the feet healthy?

A. The feet must be picked out at least twice each day and the foot checked carefully to notice its condition. The ongoing state of the shoes, if the horse is shod, should be noticed. Oiling the feet two or three times a week helps to maintain supple, healthy horn and a good appearance.

Q. What problems arise from neglect of the feet?

A. The feet may smell and then gradually become infected as a result of not being cleaned out well. Injury, owing to the presence of stones or sharp objects not removed by cleaning, may make the horse lame. Lack of observation of the condition of the shoes can lead to injury or lameness.

Horse Health

Q. How do the following headings tell us about the horse's health or ill-health?

1. **Breathing.** Breathing should be regular and quiet with a rest rate of approximately 8 to 12 breaths per minute in a healthy horse. Raised respiration without reason such as exercise or excitement, or accompanied by other signs such as sweating or pain, would indicate a possible problem with the horse's health.

2. **Eating.** A healthy horse eats consistently, confidently and thrives on his food. Changes in eating habits for no visible reason, accompanied by other worrying signs such as discomfort, change in droppings or behaviour may indicate an onset of ill-health.

3. **Excreting.** A healthy horse passes well-formed, greenish-brown droppings on a regular basis. A change in colour, consistency or smell of droppings, or more infrequent or profuse passing, may indicate the onset of ill health.

4. **Lying down.** A content, confident horse may lie down to rest. Knowing your horse's normal habits is important in assessing when there is abnormal behaviour. Resting a hind leg is quite normal, and it is usual for the horse to rest both hind legs alternately. Some horses rest a hind leg with the opposite diagonal foreleg resting too – this again is quite normal if it is something that the horse does regularly. Abnormal stance or the development of a 'new' resting habit might cause you to consider whether there was a problem. Horses can relax and sleep standing up.

5. **Moving, turning and backing.** Horses should move easily around both the field and their stable; they should turn both ways and back up as required. Any change in their ability to move confidently and with ease should be investigated.

Horse Behaviour – At Grass

Q. When feeding horses in the field, how may they behave?

A. They may move around fractiously trying to be the first to get the food; they may threaten each other with ears back and sometimes turning their hindquarters to threaten a kick in their efforts to establish superiority.

Q. What is meant by 'pecking order'?

A. The horses' desire to establish the 'head of the herd' and lower order of hierarchy by threatening each other until the lower order submit to the authority of the 'leader of the pack'. Horses lower in the pecking order will 'submit' to those above them. The term 'pecking order' comes from the behaviour shown by chickens.

Q. How do you make sure they can sort out safely their natural 'pecking order'?

A. Make sure when feeding the horses that there are more piles of food available than the number of horses, and that the food is spaced well enough apart, so that the 'boss' cannot bully the other horses away from the food. When introducing a newcomer into the group make sure that the new horse meets one or two from the group first before being put in with them all. Keep large groups of horses unshod behind so that they do not injure each other. Keep mares and geldings separately so that the 'boys' don't fight over the 'girls'.

Q. How would you know your horse was worried by flies and needed to be brought into the stable?

A. Horses running around fractiously, with visible signs of biting flies in the area of the horses. Horses in warm weather not settling and either grazing or resting in the shade. Horses showing anxiety and intermittently running about, sometimes in a quite a frenzy and disturbed state.

Horse Behaviour – In the Stable

Q. A new horse comes into the yard and is very unsettled. What precautions would you take to ensure his safety during the time he takes to settle down?

A. Keep him in a large well-bedded-down stable with nothing on which he might injure himself. Give him a plentiful supply of hay to occupy him and keep him next to another horse who is very calm and settled to try to influence the new horse. Make sure that the person looking after the horse is competent and reassuring to try to help the horse to settle. Perhaps leave stable bandages on him for protection.

Q. In what way do we go against the natural habitat of the horse when we stable him?

A. Keep him individually rather than in a herd or group.
Feed him intermittently rather than let him graze at will.
Confine him rather than allow him to wander at will.
Prevent him from exercising himself.

Restrict the interest factor in his life.

Restrict physical contact with other horses.

Q. How would you describe a nervous horse?

A. Unsettled, standing at the door looking anxious, not eating or resting calmly, may pace around the box and show disturbance whenever anything else happens in the yard.

Q. How is a nervous horse likely to react when you enter his stable?

A. He may move to the back of the box, turning his hindquarters towards you and not wishing to greet you. He may not want to be caught.

Q. How would you approach a nervous horse?

A. Calmly, with reassuring words and a quiet well-timed pat; perhaps take a small tit-bit (carrot or apple) to tempt him and show that you are friendly.

Q. What sort of things that are done to a stabled horse are likely to upset him?

A. Anything unusual or not done regularly. Possibly, clipping, treating a wound or injury, tail or mane pulling. Anything new or using equipment that is unfamiliar to him.

Q. What sort of behaviour would make you think that a horse is going to be difficult to handle in his box?

A. He goes to the back of the box when you approach.

He is miserable with ears back and a bad-tempered manner when you meet him over the door.

Difficult to catch in the box.

Bad manners or bad temper once you have the headcollar on (biting, barging, swinging his quarters towards you).

Q. What kind of behaviour in the stable would indicate that the horse when turned out might be difficult to catch?

A. Difficult to catch in the stable, anxious and timid to handle.

Q. What sort of happenings around the yard are likely to upset a stabled horse?

A. Loud or unexpected noises or sudden happenings. Another horse being removed from next door to an anxious horse.

Q. How can you calm a nervous horse?

A. Stable him next to a calm horse.

Ensure a consistent routine of management.

Spend time with him reassuring him and grooming him.

Put him in a quiet part of the yard but with other horses around him.

Have a competent, calm reassuring person to look after him.

The Horse When Ridden

Q. When being ridden, how will a horse show he is excited?

A. He may bounce or prance about, not stay relaxed and forward in a rhythm; he may try to run off.

Q. When commencing exercise, some horses will kick out. What does this behaviour demonstrate?

A. Anxiety to 'get moving'. Perhaps threatening other horses around him and invading his 'space'. Tension resulting from lack of exercise.

Q. How might your horse behave if his tack does not fit him?

(a) The saddle?

(b) The bridle?

A. (a) Reaction to a poorly fitting saddle may be shown in tension through the back when being ridden; at worst the horse may buck or try to run away; he may dip his back away when the rider mounts or just not want to go forward at all.

(b) The horse may show reluctance to go forward if the bridle is ill-fitting; if the problem is in his mouth, he may show resistance and discomfort in the mouth, and at worst he may rear. He may put his head up and avoid having the bridle put on at all.

Q. How would you behave towards your horse to get the best out of him at all times?

A. With kindness, calmness and consistency in all your actions. The horse must always understand what is being expected or asked of him. He must be rewarded often when he is genuine and accepting and corrected with understanding, firmness and clarity when he is disobedient or naughty.

STAGE 2
The Exam

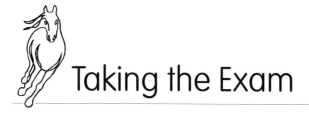# Taking the Exam

You will probably already be familiar with the protocol of a BHS exam if you have taken Stage 1. If you are coming to Stage 2 through exemption by completing Progressive Riding Tests 1 to 6 or through any other dispensation, then this may be the first BHS exam you have been involved in.

Exam psychology

- Believe in yourself and your ability to pass the exam.

- Continually remind yourself of all the preparation and practice you have put in prior to this day.

- Continually tell yourself that you will not be asked to do anything or asked a question on anything that is not totally familiar to you.

- Remember that you will know enough; you just have to show the assessors that knowledge. They cannot assume your competence or guess how much you know; you have to keep showing them and telling them.

Exam procedure

- The exam will take all day. Usually the riding on the flat and jumping takes place in the morning, followed by the lungeing. The stable management will be split into six units covering theory, practical and practical oral knowledge.

POSSIBLE
TIMETABLE/PROGRAMME
STAGE 2

15 Riding candidates
18 Care candidates

8.30	BRIEFING		
	Ride Flat/Jump	Practical/Oral	Practical
9.00	Group A	Group B	Group C
10.25	Group B	Group C	Group A
11.50	Group C	Group A	Group B
1.15	LUNCH		
	Lungeing (³/₄hr) (three horses if 20 x 60 arena available)		Theory
2.15	1–9		10–18
3.00	10–18		1–9
3.45	EXAM ENDS		

Often one section of practical stable management, one theory section and one section of riding on the flat will rotate.

- There can be up to six candidates in each stable management group; sometimes a group may be made up of candidates sitting only one or two units of the exam, while others may be taking only the riding section. There can be up to five candidates in each riding group.

- Be polite and sociable with other candidates but avoid sharing experiences. If someone tries to tell you about the horses at the centre, politely excuse yourself from the conversation. It is far better that you ride on your own initiative and competence rather than rely on snippets of information, however well meant. A small amount of isolated information about a horse may, in fact, be more of a hindrance, especially if the facts are wrong or you muddle them up with another horse. Similarly, avoid getting into conversations with other candidates who are panicking about 'how difficult the jumps are', or that 'the lunge horses are lazy', or that 'Mrs So and So is assessing and she doesn't like people with green hair and black nailpolish'! Such discussions can be damaging to your calmness and focus, and you must not get involved in them. Maintain your concentration on the day ahead and apply yourself to every situation that arises.

- If you have a bad experience in any section of the exam (e.g. a horse stops at a fence while jumping, or you drop a stable bandage halfway through applying it) stay calm and repair the situation to the best of your ability. One small mistake will never fail you, even if at the time it feels like a major catastrophe. In all cases it is the way you deal with the incident that indicates your common sense and capability (e.g. with a dropped bandage, remove the whole thing, re-roll quickly and start again).

- In every section, your assessor will introduce himself/herself and explain what he or she is expecting in that particular part of the exam. You will move around in groups of up to six, but in the practical section of the exam you will tend to be asked to carry out individual tasks or share a task with one other candidate. In the latter case make sure that you tell the assessor what parts of the work you have personally been responsible for. If you are asked to comment on something that you have not been responsible for, make sure that the assessor knows this (especially if a piece of equipment is not correctly fitted). If you have to criticise another candidate's work, do it as tactfully as possible.

- Make sure that you wear gloves when lungeing or if asked to hold a horse, but make equally sure that you remove your gloves when carrying out 'hands-on' practical tasks (e.g. grooming and fitting tack).

- Be practical and forthcoming throughout the day; relax, smile and stay comfortable (stay warm and dry, visit the loo if you need to, bring lunch and plenty of fluids to drink).

- At the end of the day make sure that you collect all your belongings, and give your arm numbers to the assessor in your final section. The results will be sent to you and should arrive within a week to ten days.

BRITISH HORSE SOCIETY EXAMINATION SYSTEM

STAGE ONE

EQL LEVEL 1 CERTIFICATE IN BHS RIDING HORSES

Riding horses on the flat and over ground poles in the light seat

EQL LEVEL 1 CERTIFICATE IN BHS HORSE KNOWLEDGE AND CARE

Brushing off horses including putting on and taking off equipment
Horse husbandry, identification and handling
The principles of caring for horses

STAGE TWO

EQL LEVEL 2 DIPLOMA IN BHS RIDING HORSES

EQL Level 2 Certificate in Riding Horses on the Flat
Ride horses on the flat in an enclosed area
Ride horses over fences in an enclosed area

EQL LEVEL 2 DIPLOMA IN BHS HORSE KNOWLEDGE AND CARE

EQL Level 2 Certificate in Horse Care
Groom and plait horses and fit equipment
The principles of horse health and anatomy
The principles of shoeing, clipping and trimming horses
Fit, remove and maintain tack for exercise
Lunge a horse under supervision

EQL Level 2 Award in the Principles of Horse Care
The principles of stabling and grassland care for horses
The principles of watering, feeding and fittening horses

STAGE THREE

EQL LEVEL 3 DIPLOMA IN BHS RIDING HORSES

EQL Level 3 Certificate in Riding Horses on the Flat
Ride horses on the flat
Ride horses over fences

EQL LEVEL 3 DIPLOMA IN BHS HORSE KNOWLEDGE AND CARE

EQL Level 3 Certificate in Horse Care
Fit tack and equipment, and care for the competition horse
Horse health, anatomy and physiology
Lunge a fit horse for exercise

EQL Level 3 Award in the Principles of Horse Care
The principles of feeding and fittening horses
The principles of stabling and grassland care for horses

To achieve the BHSAI a candidate must be successful in L3 BHS Riding Horses, L3 BHS Horse Knowledge and Care, BHS Preliminary Teaching of Horse Riding and complete a portfolio.

STAGE FOUR

BHS STAGE 4 IN RIDING HORSES ON THE FLAT

BHS STAGE 4 IN RIDING HORSES OVER FENCES

BHS STAGE 4 IN LUNGEING

Intermediate Teaching, consisting of:
Teaching riding on the flat up to BD Elementary
Teaching riding over fences, show jumping or cross-country
Teaching an improving rider on the lunge
Class lesson, either flat or grid work
Deliver a presentation
Theory covering business knowledge and teaching

To achieve BHSII a candidate must be successful in both the Stage 4 and Intermediate Teaching Test

To achieve the BHSI the candidate must be successful in BHS Stable Manager, BHS Senior Coach and BHS Equitation

RIDING AND ROAD SAFETY

EQL LEVEL 2 AWARD IN BHS RIDING HORSES SAFELY ON THE PUBLIC HIGHWAY

The principles of riding horses on the highway
Ride a horse in a enclosed area and on the highway

COACHING

EQL LEVEL 3 CERTIFICATE IN BHS PRELIMINARY TEACHING OF HORSE RIDING

Coach a group of riders for improvement
Coach an inexperienced rider for improvement

EQL Level 2 Award in the Principles of Coaching Sport
Understanding the fundamentals of coaching sport
Understanding how to develop participants
through coaching sport
Supporting participants' lifestyle through
coaching sport
Understanding the principles of safe and
equitable coaching practice

For information on UKCC Endorsed Coaching Awards and Certificates please contact the Exams Office directly for information.

EQUESTRIAN QUALIFICATIONS GB LIMITED – UNIT PROGRESSION ROUTES

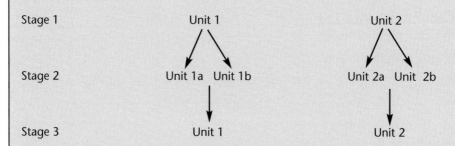

Upon achieving Unit 1 in Stage 1 Candidates may sit Unit 1a and/or Unit 1b in Stage 2

Upon achieving Unit 2 in Stage 1 Candidates may sit Unit 2a and/or Unit 2b in Stage 2

Upon achieving Unit 3 in Stage 1 Candidates may sit Unit 3a and/or Unit 3b in Stage 2

Candidates must achieve Unit 1a and Unit 1b in Stage 2 to progress to Unit 1 in Stage 3

Candidates must achieve Units 2a and Unit 2b in Stage 2 to Progress to Unit 2 in Stage 3

Candidates must achieve Unit 3a in Stage 2 in order to sit Unit 3a in Stage 3

Candidates must achieve Unit 3b in Stage 2 in order to sit Unit 3b in Stage 3

Candidates must achieve Unit 4 in Stage 2 to progress Unit 4 in Stage 3

Candidates must achieve Stage 1 riding to progress to Stage 2 riding on the flat. Candidates may apply to sit both the riding on the flat and jumping in Stage 2 but must pass Stage 2 on the flat in order to progress to Stage 2 in the jumping. Upon successful completion of Stage 2 jumping, candidates may apply to sit the Stage 3 riding on the flat and jumping. They may only progress to the jumping section if they are successful in the flat.

Candidates may follow the riding on the flat route without jumping. Candidates who are successful on the flat may apply to sit the jumping section at a later date if they prefer.

Preliminary Teaching Test:

Candidates may apply for the principle (theory) units without any prerequisite qualifications.
In order to apply for the two practical units i.e. coach a group of riders for improvement and/or coach an inexperienced rider for improvement candidates must hold the following:

> EQL Level 1 Certificate in Riding Horses
> EQL level 1 Certificate in BHS Horse Knowledge and Care
> EQL Level 2 Diploma in BHS Riding Horses
> EQL level 2 Diploma in BHS Horse Knowledge and Care

Direct Entry routes are available in exceptional circumstances; please contact the Examinations Office for details

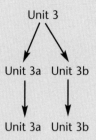

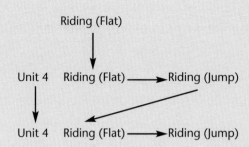

Unit 3

Unit 3a   Unit 3b

Unit 3a   Unit 3b

Riding (Flat)

Unit 4   Riding (Flat) ⟶ Riding (Jump)

Unit 4   Riding (Flat) ⟶ Riding (Jump)

Stage 1: Unit 1   Brushing off Horses Including Putting On and Taking off Equipment
Unit 2 = Horse Husbandry, Identification and Handling
Unit 3 = The Principles of Caring for Horses
Riding = Riding Horses on the Flat and Over Ground Poles in the Light Seat

Stage 2: Unit 1a   Groom and Plait Horses and Fit Equipment
Unit 1b = Fit, Remove and Maintain Tack for Exercise
Unit 2a = The Principles of Horse Health and Anatomy
Unit 2b = The Principles of Shoeing, Clipping and Trimming Horses
Unit 3a = The Principles of Watering, Feeding and Fittening Horses
Unit 3b = The Principles of Stabling and Grassland Care for Horses
Unit 4 = Lunge a Horse Under Supervision
Flat = Ride Horses on the Flat in an Enclosed Area
Jumping = Ride Horses Over Fences in an Enclosed Area

Stage 3: Unit 1   Fit Tack and Equipment and Care for the Competition Horse
Unit 2 = Horse Health, Anatomy and Physiology
Unit 3a = The Principles of Feeding and Fittening Horses
Unit 3b = The Principles of Stabling and Grassland Care for Horses
Unit 4 = Lunge a Fit Horse for Exercise
Flat = Ride Horses on the Flat
Jumping = Ride Horses over Fences

Further Reading

The following books and booklets can all be obtained from the BHS Bookshop.

The BHS Complete Manual of Horse and Stable Management

The BHS Veterinary Manual Second Edition

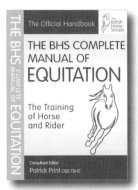

The BHS Complete Manual of Equitation

The BHS Training Manual for Progressive Riding Tests 1-6

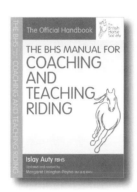

**The BHS Manual for
Coaching and
Teaching Riding**

**The BHS Riding and
Road Safety Manual –
Riding and Roadcraft**

The BHS Stage 2 Workbook

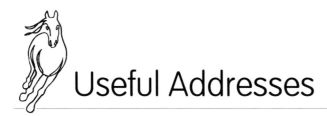

Useful Addresses

The British Horse Society
Abbey Park
Stareton
Kenilworth
Warwickshire
CV8 2XZ
tel: 02476 840500
fax: 02476 840501
website: www.bhs.org.uk
email: enquiry@bhs.org.uk

BHS Standards Directorate

BHS Examinations Department
Abbey Park
Stareton
Kenilworth
Warwickshire
CV8 2XZ
tel: 02476 840508
email: exams@bhs.org.uk

BHS Training Department
Abbey Park
Stareton
Kenilworth
Warwickshire
CV8 2XZ
tel: 02476 840507
email: training@bhs.org.uk

BHS Riding Schools/Approvals Department
Abbey Park
Stareton
Kenilworth
Warwickshire
CV8 2XZ
tel: 02476 840509
email: Riding.Schools@bhs.org.uk